8 GREAT WONDERS

"WHAT DO THESE STORIES HAVE TO DO WITH US?"

ERIC HOLMES

xulon
PRESS

8 Great Wonders: "What Do These Stories Have to Do with Us?"

by Eric Holmes

Printed in the United States of America

ISBN 1-60034-626-X

To the memory of my dad, Roger E. Holmes *1939 - 1993*, whose influence appears on most every page.

www.xulonpress.com

TABLE OF CONTENTS

Prologue

page vii   ❧ The Front Page

Part I – View the Forest

page 1   1 ❧ What's It All About?

Part II – Study the Maps

page 13   2 ❧ What Could Have Been, Will Be
page 27   3 ❧ Separated, Condemned, Executed
page 41   4 ❧ Death = Death, Life = Life
page 52   Resolution in a Weekend?
page 54   Celebration for a Life
page 59   5 ❧ Spirit, Soul, and Body
page 75   6 ❧ Before We Break Camp

Part III – Follow the Path

page 85   7 ❧ God Creates People.................................... *1st Great Wonder*
page 103   8 ❧ People Sin Against God.............................. *2nd Great Wonder*
page 121   9 ❧ God's Law Is Given.................................... *3rd Great Wonder*
page 139   10 ❧ Jesus Christ Dies .... *4th Great Wonder*
page 153   11 ❧ Jesus, Alive Again! .... *5th Great Wonder*
page 173   12 ❧ <u>your name</u> Accepts Salvation .... *6th Great Wonder*
page 195   13 ❧ <u>your name</u> Lives by Faith............................ *7th Great Wonder*
page 217   14 ❧ God and People, Together Forever.................. *8th Great Wonder*

Epilogue

page 231   ❧ Some People Reject God

❧ Acknowledgements

I wrote the original edition of *8 Great Wonders* very quickly; five drafts in just five months. It was my baby and I was one proud papa. But when we released the book, something happened that I wasn't expecting. People who read it on their own didn't seem to get much out of it, but people who were attending our courses were getting excited about what they were experiencing. *How could that happen? It was the same book!*

I discovered that the difference was, when I taught the material live, I added personal stuff—stories, analogies, testimonies—stuff I didn't write into the book. I realized that the book was nothing more than a technical manual, and few people actually enjoy reading tech manuals.

This "stories, analogies, testimonies" edition of *8 Great Wonders* took 22 months to write and is the result of the efforts of a very special team of people.

First, I want to thank my beautiful wife Francine and my wonderful daughter Holly. You mean the world to me. I want to thank my mom Nancy, and my sister Chris, who, like Fran and Holly, gave me their love, support, prayers, patience, involvement, feedback, and encouragement. I love you all very much.

Thank you, Sam Allred and Brian Rothove, for your support and encouragement as friends, and for your leadership as ministry directors. I also appreciate your patience as I immersed myself in the writing process.

I want to thank the members of our ministry's creative brainstorming team—Julie, Ken, Leesa, and Terry—and their families as well. You guys are much more than just a design editor, an actor, a poet, and a musician. I'm deeply indebted to you.

I greatly appreciate all of you who have supported the ministry and my family through your prayers and your contributions. I'll never be able to express how much it means to me to have friends who believe so strongly in what we're doing.

Special thanks to Danny and Angie Fulham, and their family.

Special thanks to Ginger Mead, a woman of prayer who told me in no uncertain terms that she would *not* let me give up.

Special thanks to Julie Hawkins, and Ken and Cindy Morris, who not only brainstormed, but prayed, held me accountable, and proofread the manuscript several times.

And special thanks to Elizabeth Laurie, a professional writer and editor who helped carry us across the finish line. You were an answer to prayer at exactly the right moment.

Last, but in no way least, I want to offer a very important thank you to the individuals who took a risk and participated in one of the first eleven courses we held (some more than once): Allen, Amy, Angie, Becky, Bill, Brandon, Brian, Carolyn, Charlene, Chris, Christopher, Cindy, Connie, Craig, Danielle, David, Delton, Diana C, Diana J, Dustin M, Dustin W, Elizabeth, Francine, Ginger, Grant, Holly H, Holly L, Julie, Ken, Kent, Leesa, Lloyd, Mary, Melissa, Michael, Nancy, Robert, Ron, Ryan, Sam, Sarah, Shannon, Shari, Steve, Teresa H, Teresa M, Tim, and Tina.

❧ The Front Page

I asked someone to explain the difference between a foreword, a preface, and an introduction in a book. He thought it was the same difference as a sofa, a couch, and a divan. Then I treated him to dinner, or was it supper? In other words, all of us are the same. But different.

I'm about to accuse you of being on a search for truth. Everyone is. Of course, you would have to tell me whether it's barely a search, an earnest search, or something in between. I'm pretty sure that none of us want to be lied to. Raise your right hand if you want to build your life on something you know is wrong. See? We're the same.

Here's an insignificant speck of truth: I never get excited about contests. Except that one time.

Searching for Gold Spike

My hometown newspaper ran one of those hide-and-seek contests. They called it *Gold Spike*. What they did was hide several gold-colored railroad spikes around town. Then, each day for a week, they published clues which could lead searchers to a certain spike. It certainly sounded simple enough, but who wants to get in their car and drive all over God's green earth looking for a small object, especially in October when there's a chill in the air? Not me. Even after seeing the list of amazing products, services, and gift certificates that local merchants were offering as prizes, I still wasn't in.

But when I saw the first clue my heart began pounding.

- *Lipton Tea could be on ice. Famous American hero took off from here, has soared with the stars, and will soar again.*

Why in the world would this excite me?

There are several airports in Johnson County, Kansas, but only one had a Lipton Tea facility nearby; the Industrial Airport. The Industrial Airport was originally the Olathe Naval Air Station. And I grew up living in the housing complex that naval officers and their families once called home. I spent most of my teen years walking, exploring, and writing songs at the airport in this very clue. Basically, the spike was in my own backyard. It was as good as mine.

The next clue was published the following day, and a newspaper was in my hot little hands bright and early.

- *Take a stroll down memory lane and salute Dixie Keefer, Roberds, and Coulter. When in the park, switch over to the starboard side.*

This is too easy! Immediately, I was in my car racing to a little memorial park where some old Navy planes are on display. I figured I was the only person who knew that there are three old street signs from the Naval Air days lining the walkway. The street names, of course, were *Dixie Keefer*, *Roberds*, and *Coulter*.

I parked my car and saw that there were already a half a dozen people combing the area with metal detectors, Geiger counters, and bomb-sniffing dogs. Okay, so it was only a lady holding her French poodle. How dare they look for my spike!

I joined them, none of us speaking a single word. I know we covered every square inch of that park, but no one found the spike that day.

I had definitely been bitten by the *Gold Spike* bug, and competition only worsened my condition. I would spend time in the park before I went to work, during my lunch hours, and before I went home each evening. I was determined to find this spike and claim my prizes.

It was still dark outside when I picked up Wednesday's paper.

- *Many strategies have been planned above me. Lots of alcohol spilt on me. Come on in about 60 feet. Sorry, no seats.*

The wheels began turning. *Strategies are planned and carried out from the cockpits of jets—jets which probably use some kind of alcohol-based fuel. The two jets in the park are within 60 feet of each other, and the cockpits are sealed shut; no way to get to the seats.* I just knew that I would find the spike somewhere between the cockpit and the fuel tank of one of those jets. But, believe me, it wasn't anywhere near the planes.

I grabbed Thursday's paper and read, thankfully, that the spike still hadn't been found.

Morning: dozens of people in the park; no spike.

Midday: more people in the park; still no spike.

Evening: just a few of us; looking for the elusive spike as the sun went down.

So there I stood; at the Industrial Airport, several blocks from the Lipton Tea facility, inside the memorial park, about 60 feet from one of the jets. I was scouring the ground an inch at a time. That's when it happened. I still have it today. I reached down and picked up a spike; a dirty, old, rusty railroad spike—a spike that wasn't gold.

I scratched it real hard. Maybe there was gold coloring underneath. No. Just more rust.

The clues have led me to this spike, I thought. *I know they have. Maybe I'm supposed to take this spike to the newspaper office and exchange it for the gold one.*

But that's not how the rules of the contest read.

This just has to be it. But why isn't it gold?

Friday's paper announced that the spike had indeed been found—but not by me. Where was it? Did you notice that I brushed right by one of the clues? *When in the park, switch over to the starboard side.* The real gold spike was just across the street from the park where so many of us had been searching. It was where the Naval Officer's Club used to stand—*strategies planned, alcohol spilt, no seats.*

When I think back to that contest, it suggests to me that people still search for spikes. But not the kind hidden by contest committees. Today we search for gold spikes of truth. Like I said before, some of us barely search, while others earnestly search. And, you know, some of us already hold some kind of truth in our hands. Question is: Is it gold or is it rusty?

My Own Search and Discovery

My own search, a *desperate quest* for truth, was born out of a family crisis. It began on May 14th, 1991, when I was forced to recognize that what I already held in my hands was rusty.

My dad had been rushed to the emergency room. Doctors were telling us that he was as close to death as a person could come and still be alive. How could this happen? I was raised believing in the Christian doctrine of divine healing. *It is always God's will to heal his people of sickness and disease.* No one in my immediate family had seen a doctor for anything other than school physicals in more than 20 years. None of us needed to. I had personally experienced healing in my life many times—and in some cases miraculously. How could disease be claiming my dad's life when there was so much thought and doctrine behind our beliefs? How was it possible that reality could crush my theology? But that's exactly what was happening.

As I waited outside for my sister to arrive at the hospital, I was trying to figure out what God could be up to. It didn't take long for me to come to the end of myself. Knowing the problem was on my side—not God's—I prayed a different kind of prayer.

Something has gone wrong, and it has everything to do with what I believe. I literally held an open hand up to him. *Show me how everything fits together. Show me the truth.*

What followed was an amazing time in my life as God properly connected the puzzle pieces of Christianity for me. I praised him out loud as I learned about his grace; his overwhelming love for me. I shed tears as he spoke to me about my faith; my belief and obedience, not only to what he *has said* in the Bible, but also to what he *says* to me today. And I saw a deepening of my understanding of salvation, with its different effects on every part of me—spirit, soul, and body. Despite the hardship of my dad's recovery efforts, it was the most exciting time of my life.

The funny thing is that God didn't give me a new set of beliefs or activities. Instead, it was as if he said, *Allow me to show you what a friendship with me really looks like.*

For quite awhile I really couldn't have explained what it was that God had taught me exactly. But one morning, about 16 months after my "show me how everything fits together" prayer at the hospital, the 10 and 11 year olds in my Sunday school class responded to that day's lesson with a question.

"What do these stories have to do with us?"

I knew it was an important question at a vital time in these kids' lives.

I fumbled around for an instant answer, but it certainly didn't satisfy them ... or me. The following Sunday, before class, I prayed for a way to communicate the very real connection between the events of the Bible and our lives. *God, how do I teach these kids the truths you've taught me?* I began listing Bible stories across the chalkboard: Creation, Sin, The Ten Commandments, The Death of Jesus Christ, His Resurrection, My Salvation, My Life as a Christian, and Heaven.

I taught the lesson that morning moving back and forth between those eight events. For 45 minutes I pointed, questioned, joked, underlined, explained, called on raised hands, told personal stories—I might have even sang and danced a little. When it was over, I was amazed at how the kids seemed to understand and be satisfied. And once the class was dismissed and the room had cleared, I copied everything on that chalkboard like a madman. God had answered my prayer, and then some.

Now most of my 'good ideas' for teaching talks or Bible studies end up in a file drawer in my basement. But these eight events kept kicking around in my head. I found myself doodling illustrations for them between calls at my job. I made it a game to come up with new ways to describe these events without using ideas I had thought of before. And one day this grandiose title came to me: *The 8 Great Wonders of Human History.* Just between you and me, I thought it was about the most over-the-top thing I had ever heard. Although, somehow it felt right.

Looking back, I would have to say that for awhile I treated the whole concept as more of a hobby. But in the middle of a cold December night in 1993, I had to take it very seriously.

My dad always said that he didn't want to be eulogized at his funeral. He wanted the gospel of Jesus Christ to be preached instead. He was adamant about it. And so the *8 Great Wonders* became a sermon for the first time, the day after Christmas. Preaching, rather than eulogizing, was the most difficult thing I've ever done in my life.

Later, the sermon became a series of eight church talks. The handouts I gave everyone were 14 pages long, although it was mostly space to write down opinions and answers.

For a total of 11 years, the project just kept growing. The handouts were expanded as pertinent Bible studies were completed. From time to time stories and analogies were added. Once, I even conducted an informal survey via the Internet with more than 50 people from different Christian backgrounds. I found that, although we Christians read the same Scriptures, we give different meanings to the words we read. The data fit right into the developing material. Despite the serious-sounding nature of my survey, not one time in all those years did I ever see the *8 Great Wonders* as anything more than a personal project.

Then, in May 2003, the craziest thought occurred to me: *Why don't you start your own ministry?* My next thought was, *Yeah, right. Like that'll happen.* Sam and another friend were there in the room with me. They're both down-to-earth, no-nonsense types, so I figured I would ask them and they would certainly tell me how crazy the thought really was. But I heard God say, *Just Sam.* (I should have known something was up.)

I couldn't believe what I was hearing next. "Eric," Sam said, "God told me a week ago that I would help someone start a ministry. Brother, it's you."

Once the shock wore off, I described for Sam the only possible project I had (maybe) which we might actually be able to build a Christian ministry around (kind of)—*8 Great Wonders.*

Work began as I wrote these eight events into mock headlines and newspaper stories. And five months later, in January 2004, we released our 78-page workbook.

8 Great Wonders

At this point, a couple of basic questions might be coming to mind. *So what are the '8 Great Wonders' anyway? And what makes these alleged wonders so great?* (A couple of smart alecks I know have also asked, "How do you know there aren't nine wonders?") I consider an event to be a great wonder when it has met two simple qualifications. First, when the event took place it had to have had a real effect on the entire human race, no exceptions. And second, the event has to have the potential to impact individual lives today as well.

The dramatic events of secular history are announced in headlines every day. As time passes, we tend to remember these moments by their headlines. For example, *Terrorists Attack America.* We know the stories from September 11th, 2001 and we remember exactly where we were and what we were doing when we heard what was happening. More importantly, we know how it affected our lives.

As far as I can tell, the eight greatest moments in God's history with people have never appeared in newsprint. And so, without further adieu, let me present the most impacting headlines since time began:

- ***God Creates People***
  After creating airborne and aquatic animals yesterday, God continued to display his mastery over the physical sciences ...

- ***People Sin Against God***

  Details are sketchy, but something seems to have gone very wrong in paradise. The Garden of Eden was shut down this afternoon …

- ***God's Law Is Given***

  For the third time is as many days, Israel's leader, Moses, has met directly with God himself. In the two prior meetings, the pair …

- ***Jesus Christ Dies***

  Never has a Roman execution attracted so much attention. Jesus of Nazareth, a self-styled Jewish teacher, was crucified …

- ***Jesus, Alive Again!***

  Very early this morning, controversy erupted when the tomb containing the dead body of Jesus of Nazareth was found empty.

Rather than writing 'a person' or 'an individual' in the following blanks, I want us to personalize these next two events with our own first and last names. Go ahead and write your own.

- _____ _____ ***Accepts Salvation***

- _____ _____ ***Lives by Faith***

The eighth and final headline reads:

- ***God and People, Together Forever***

  Science-fiction writers could not have crafted a more incredible story than what the world has been witnessing …

"What do these stories have to do with us?"

For many people I've spoken with, it's as though they were once offered a box of puzzle pieces called Christianity and told to make sense of it all. But even now, they silently ask the same question my Sunday school kids had asked. *What do these stories have to do with me?*

By the time we've finished looking at God's history with people, we'll have a better understanding of what the reality of Christianity is all about, why it's important, and how we can truly experience it for ourselves.

The *8 Great Wonders* message will come in three parts, moving from *interesting*, to *challenging*, to *impacting*.

Part I, the first chapter only, is presented with *interest* in mind. It's an overview of what the *8 Great Wonders* material is all about. Picture us in an airplane at 30,000 feet. We're flying over the search site. Now look out your window. What you see below us is the forest where the adventure will take place. We have to see the forest to understand the trees. It's important to keep the big picture in mind as we proceed through the rest of the book.

Part II, primarily Chapter 2 through Chapter 5, *challenges* the way we may have seen Christianity in the past. We'll see the connections between certain 'great wonders,' as though guides were mapping out our trek before we begin. These maps for the journey show us the ultimate goal, the fatal dangers, an unbelievable rescue, and the escape to safety. Part II ends with Chapter 6, which is a bridge between challenge and impact. Imagine being handed someone's personal journal the day before the trek begins. It's written by someone who has already experienced much of what the forest has to offer. Something like that could not only help us; it could save our lives.

Part III, Chapters 7 through 14, is designed to be *impacting*. We'll take a look at each of the *8 Great Wonders*, one at a time. A Christian could actually deepen his or her life of faith via the events we will be covering.

I'm convinced that these *8 Great Wonders* can impact us. But have you ever noticed how the things that ultimately impact us seem to challenge us first?

We can all be *impacted* through our experiences with God. But are you willing to be *challenged* by him?

I'm sure that this message will be challenging for some. Will *you* be one of the ones who are impacted?

There are questions at the end of each of these 14 chapters which can prompt deeper thought about the message. Although many individuals will answer the questions on their own, I want to suggest that it might be more beneficial to gather with other people and go through the *8 Great Wonders* as part of a book discussion group.

Now, I'll admit that in the past I've been guilty of doing Bible studies this way. I open the Bible, read a few interesting verses, and then walk away, leaving the lessons behind. But what we're talking about here comes from a question deep in our hearts:

What do these stories have to do with us?

We can't afford to leave the lessons in the book.

When my wife and I first started hosting discussion groups for the *8 Great Wonders*, I came up with a contest called *Search & Rescue*. It's loosely based on the idea of a search for the *Gold Spike*.

Each week, group members who chose to participate (not everyone did) received points for extra effort. At the end of our discussion time, they would give themselves:

- **4 points** if they read the chapter ahead of time
- **8 points** if they answered questions at the end of the chapter
- **1 point** if they noted a recent news story that related to the topic
- **2 points** if they noted a personal story that related to the topic
- **16 points** if they wrote down something that impacted them, either as they read or as we discussed the chapter together

The person with the highest score was named 'Searcher' of the week. And the person who was named Searcher for the most weeks total was crowned 'Rescuer.'

Right up front I told our group that a contest like this for grown-ups was pretty goofy. I told them plainly that my intention was to 'trick' them into taking the *8 Great Wonders* more seriously than they otherwise would have. Six of the ten group members participated in our competition, and each of them was named Searcher at least once. More importantly, when we met for the final session all ten of the participants shared something that they gained from the message—not *learned*, but *gained*.

What is it that you could gain? Are you ready to join the search party?

Then grab a pen. I know that God will bless you in your discoveries.

Eric

```
D A H C S S T A D S E E N O R O O O H R R V H E L R R N W S T O
T E Y R N E A S E E U J R I T E C H H T A E A W W E O H E E S D
L D E A U O J W I H H S D A G E W E R W D E T S E N H F C E N O
R O N N D O C D T R D T E O E E L E W E E O W E E S E T N S B D
A C T A Y E N E I I H E M J G W B B W F G I G Y T B U H N A U E
V B E S M L N I R D T C G O S E D S A P I N H Y H U L A W A L S
E A E H U I E O E D M U S N R W R E I S I E O T E W O L C N C P
A J H H T S H T M V N E B U A F E O T H I H F L E B M H I E I E
N S H E T N E W A I E A H N S H E N F A S R S I O L O O G W B S
F O A G W S O J O R H I D T E E C S D E R N E D L N Y S R U E S
U O O H U E N D H N E Y L E F V J A O O B A A H N S S R I F O W
D E D N D O C I E T K P B E I O I F S R O Y P L C E I I E D E R
H A V L O O R N S I A O S N B F E G O E E G T E P A I H D T O M
O T E A R T G H O R D E T E W D I N S L C H E L S R E R Y N L T
E C D D S O P Y T D U S D E D O N T O A E U T H I R E T F B A U
D S E O E T W U L D A O U O L O N A S N W P D A T U A H S E D F
L A O V G H O E E E O E L S T P S K S U E W S O H M G F T U H E
V E N H A H T N R V T G D L E S O E E U J N A O R T I G W O O T
P A S I C H T M S I I E H E A J R E W B S E O L G P T H N O E I
G O S M T E E I O E T L L T H N N E P N D E R T S E D C H I H K
I I L E I H V W W R O N O P I T E E N D O N J E S D H O A T D S
U L L E B H G E E E F D E T M W M V H N E I A D W T O T G F I N
A S E E V O O U D R B M T E D O P O I W I T T D R E S G G H E W
D T W R R E T T A N E L I A H R C I R G Y S A A O O W R M N T H
T E S O U R D D D C A H L H H T A S H F R T S E V G L S I I I I
W N I E H T E O E L N M W I D T D D N S S O L N R L W E U F H O
G P O D S S U H T E R A A W W E T E N O N U F A M C A O H T E M
O E I D E U D F T E N O M D O S S U T A I O E S N E D S N T S H
T R R H E W C N A O L D W O A N U I B C T T I S A E D O E K H N
I T F A S S S X A D O B N E W N K S A S I S S T I H P N G H N T
U A S D E N A U E N N N A A H E E O E R U V A E A A D H O G T A
C O G A E W O B R T I A F E M T H H T J S S N E U L R O T C N S
U E M A C T E I S O U S E L R I D T W T N A E O B Q E O G A W I
N E W R S N A R T I F O R P E A H E F M N I H J C O E R T D E A
L N V R U N I R E A N D H U O S E H L O I A S D H S T S A S N D
R E I I O O I S A H L O E T O H R W T I S H T R O G G T O R T A
S U H G G F H S T P W E I I I S A U N I C R Y R E G U N N H E N
A U O T E D D T R U E D R T D W L S O I W N E B O V T O I A T D
I W R D D B N E I U O S N R A S E A E Y A D O S N P E A R H E S
R S D O I O E A T W O H E A U V U R E V R G E C U W M I H H C M
R E N N F A G H R A S G T R E O L S E V I O A I E C O I L T T A
E E W O A D P M T E E S N I E R Y A E W E L F N D R C N S E T D
E T V S C D E S O T F R E I W W E T S J L R R T R E D A K I B R
A L S E N T A I U R A F C F D S Y H I D N L W U S O W O E E T L
L E I U N A R E D S F S O E N L I E E N E E A A O I B S G H B I
```

1 &❧; What's It All About?

"Shh."

"What's up?"

"It's a debate between an atheist and a Christian. The atheist is the one speaking now."

The View from an Atheist

I am also concerned because the standard that the Christian God sets for everyone seems too unreasonably high.

Remember, we are discussing a Christian God here. To believe in a Christian God means that you have to accept many additional ideas, beyond that of a Creator. Most notably, you have to believe that Jesus was actually God.

Look at the concept of loving your brother as you love yourself. Can you take seriously the concept of loving all other human beings with the same strong, heart-felt desire to help, the same thought and compassion as you love yourself? If you even consider the possibility, you will realize that your life has to dramatically change. You cannot continue to live in your dream home, or drive your luxury car to your job everyday. You cannot continue to adore your spouse and your children more than anyone else in the world. No. Loving your brother makes a much higher demand on you. Not only do you have to care for your fellow man as much as you care for your family, you have to care for him as much as you care for yourself. All those selfish dreams you have, all those selfish plans you make; you cannot do those things for you anymore. You have to be diligent to care for all other human beings instead.

Just try taking all this seriously.

You aren't doing it. I'm not either. I sincerely wish I could. I don't even think the Mahatma Gandhi was able to do it. Maybe one person was able to live that kind of selflessness—Christ himself, if we can even take the idea of Christ seriously.

But if 'you' are going to take the idea of Christ seriously, then you need to be ready to turn your life upside-down ... or feel like a failure in living up to the standard that Christ has set for you. And, quite frankly, I don't know that any of us here are moral failures. From what I see, we're doing a fairly nice job of living decent lives, despite failing to live up to this higher moral demand, this cause for dramatic transformation.

So I believe, unfortunately for people, that the Christian God sets the standard too unreasonably high.

We've just heard the thoughts of an atheist[1]. An atheist is a person who is convinced that God does not exist. (It may also be important to note that someone who is an agnostic isn't sure one way or the other. The question of God's existence is an important one to them. They just haven't seen a conclusive answer.)

What thought process leads someone to conclude that God does not exist?

I've talked with two or three people who claimed to be atheists, and I've listened, a number of times, to radio programs hosted by *free-thinkers*, but my curiosity has never been satisfied. How does a person become convinced that there is no God? What thought process brings them to this conclusion?

I tagged along with my nephew's church youth group to see the debate between the atheist paraphrased above and a Christian. Actually, the spokesman for the atheistic view said at one point that he wouldn't consider himself to be an atheist. He was just someone who *doubted* the existence of the Christian God.

As debates go, it was a fairly good one. Both men were articulate and handled themselves well, but I would have to say that neither participant delivered what could be considered a knockout punch. Despite being a Christian myself and agreeing with the Christian arguments, I would have to call it a draw.

I did come away from the event with an important thought. I'm not sure that a debate is the proper platform for Christianity. One professor argued the points of Christianity. But within the other professor's opposing points, I heard questions which could, and should, be answered. Nietzsche, Voltaire, and Marx have influenced cultures and hearts for many years with the 'dark godlessness' found in the books they have written. But it occurred to me after the debate: if their theories produce these questions for atheists, then atheism really can't be intimidating at all. Atheism is simply a series of questions which haven't been answered yet.

The View from Most Christians

NOTES

At this point, you may expect me to proclaim "Christianity rocks," or something like that. However, there's a lot to suggest that the Christian religion might not be what it's cracked up to be. There seems to be an 'unknown' or 'ignored' quality to it for many who claim to be Christians.

For instance, I was on the phone with a friend who surprised me by saying, "Christianity has a wonderfully mysterious quality to it. I don't think we can really know the truth regarding its teachings." Because of this, he resists sharing his views on anything biblical.

I've also discovered that, statistically, most Christian 'believers' don't believe like we might assume they do.

George Barna is a Christian pollster. His research often shows "a radical gap between what we heard Christians professing they believed and the values and the lifestyle that grew out of the values[2]."

I remember the first time I logged on to *The Barna Group* web site[3] and read through the statistics in their archives. I literally felt sick in the pit in my stomach and was on the verge of tears. But rather than rattling off numbers to you, I want to take you through a few of the questions[4] which thousands have answered.

Here's the first question. *Do you consider yourself a deeply spiritual person?* The response: *Sixty-two percent (62%) of Americans answer 'yes.'*

Do you feel accepted by God? Eighty-eight percent (88%) of Americans answer 'yes.'

Do you believe you have a clear, personal understanding of the meaning and purpose of your life? Eighty-two percent (82%) of Americans answer 'yes.'

Do you consider yourself to be Christian? Based on these numbers and more, we know absolutely that most Americans do.

Do you base your moral decisions on the Bible? I was caught off guard by the response: *Only sixteen (16%) percent of people answer 'yes.'*

The Barna Group also asks eight questions which they feel determine whether or not a Christian possesses what's known as a *biblical worldview*. How would you answer these questions?

Do you believe that absolute moral truth exists?[5] .... Yes / No

Do you believe that the source of moral truth is the Bible?[6] .... Yes / No

Do you believe that the Bible is accurate

    in all of the principles it teaches?[7] .... Yes / No

Do you believe that Jesus Christ lived a sinless life on earth?[8] .... Yes / No

Do you believe that eternal salvation can be earned?[9] .... Yes / No

Do you believe that every person has a responsibility

    to share their religious beliefs with others?[10] .... Yes / No

Do you believe that Satan is a living force,

    not just a symbol of evil?[11] .... Yes / No

Do you believe that God is the all-knowing, all-powerful

    maker of the universe who still rules that creation today?[12] .... Yes / No

Would you like to guess the outcome of the survey in light of these eight questions? *Only five percent (5%) of adults have a biblical worldview.* I wonder if our atheist friend would call these people 'practical doubters' rather than 'true believers.'

If I was an atheist I think this would be one of my proofs that Christianity is a farce. But I'm not an atheist; I'm a Christian. Christianity isn't a question mark that I ignore. It makes sense to me. It's the most logical, practical, reasonable thing I've ever experienced. As my friend on the phone suggested, there is a sense of the unknown to being a Christian. But it's not found in the area of Bible teaching or doctrine. It's found in the uniqueness of a personal relationship with God.

It's All About Relationship

Maybe you're like me and you've lost count of how many times you've heard the statement *Christianity is a relationship, not a religion.* I've lost track of how many times I've said it. But it seems that the word *relationship*, when applied to God and me, doesn't mean the same thing as when it's applied to marriage, friendships, or even neighbors. What conclusion would a psychologist draw if they measured our friendship with God by the qualities needed for all other healthy human relationships? Being related *to* someone—as in, "God is our

Father, we are his children"—isn't necessarily the same thing as being in a relationship *with* someone. Maybe I can demonstrate the point this way.

My wife was born into the world Francine Mary Adam on a spring day in Chicago, Illinois. Her father Abe was from Syria. Her mother Marietta is 100% Italian. Francine's hair is black. Her skin is olive. And as a couple of strangers have pointed out, she has subtle Middle Eastern features.

Abe and Marietta had two other daughters, Mary and Charlene, before they were divorced. Francine is the oldest of the three girls. When she was six years old, she and her two sisters were adopted by their step-father Dan. Dan and Marietta's marriage produced a baby sister, Teresa. Dan died of cancer many years later. Marietta and her four daughters are part of a close-knit Italian family.

> Can a person be *related* to someone without being in a *relationship* with them?

Francine became a Christian on July 19th, 1973. She remembers the night like it was yesterday evening. It happened during a Bible study in her cousin's living room, and was one of the most exciting and joy-filled decisions she has ever made. Unfortunately, no one in the family who had accepted Christ as Savior ever became connected to a local church. No seasoned Christian ever came along to show any of them what it really means to live as a Christian. And before long, all of them had drifted into a lifestyle of partying, Francine included.

By 1982, Francine was living a double-life—responsible office manager and 'nice girl' at work, a drug dealer's girlfriend living on an emotional roller coaster at home. At one point, she found herself kneeling in the bathroom, asking God to get her out of this mess of a situation. Matters grew worse.

Rock bottom came when Francine's boyfriend died of a brain aneurism. He was just 30 years old. It was a shocking wake-up call, which also led to one of Francine's closest friends becoming a Christian. Francine began attending Willow Creek Community Church in South Barrington, Illinois, where she began to grow as a Christian under the teaching of Bill Hybels and others.

Francine is an emotionally sensitive woman. She shines when everyone is happy. She's an awesome cook, so happiness comes to everyone she serves. She's a woman of compassion, a person of prayer. She's a giver like you wouldn't believe. She's a loving mother, a devoted wife, a committed Christian.

Now here's the question. Have I said anything that indicates that Francine and I have a solid relationship?

"Well, Eric, you did refer to her as your wife, and you seem to know a lot about her."

What if I had written a similar-type biography of my favorite singer, Elvis Presley, a person I never met, rather than my wife?

"Well, Eric, you did refer to him as your favorite singer, and you seem to know a lot about him."

Sure, the fact that Francine and I are married indicates that we're *related*, but it doesn't prove that we've built a *relationship* that consists of mutual respect, or that we communicate, or that there are shared experiences that have drawn us closer personally.

Again, many people refer to God as their heavenly Father. We can know a lot about him through the teachings of Jesus. But this alone doesn't prove that we know him, that he speaks to us, and that he's interactive in our lives.

Does it seem odd that God speaks to people?

Dr. Thomas Szasz once noted the common misconception that "If you talk to God, you are praying. If God talks to you, you have schizophrenia.[13]" I've run into this notion myself as I've shared stories of what God has done in my life and what he has spoken to me. More than once a Christian friend has responded, "What do you mean God talks to you?"

Here's an example of what I mean.

Francine had been living in Olathe only a couple of years when we met. I was a visitor to her church's singles group. I was attracted to her the very first time I saw her, but immediately, God told me that physical attraction isn't the basis for the relationships he develops. I spent a number of months building a friendship with Francine and the others in the group, thinking that this was as far as it would ever go between us.

Later, I became very concerned when I learned that Francine was scheduled for an out-patient surgical procedure. I spent an afternoon with her and her roommate, hoping to support her through this tough time. It turns out I was the one needing the emotional boost. She was perfectly fine. As I left her apartment that day, God said, *This is what my relationships are based on; a true caring for the person.*

Now this is all sweet and sentimental, and what else would you expect a Christian couple to claim about the beginnings of their romance? But what I've just shared with you is simply the set-up for something else, something completely unexpected.

I was sitting next to Francine, with the other singles in the group, at a Saturday night church service. Two men spoke that night, one of them claiming to be a 'prophet.' Now the idea of a prophet standing right in front of me wasn't a part of my background as a Christian, so I was a little skeptical—actually, a lot skeptical. But I was willing to listen with as open a mind as I could muster.

The prophet spoke of a vision he had seen within the previous few days. An angel had shown him around heaven. At one point in his story, it seemed that everyone in the room gasped together in amazement. I was finding all of this hard to believe, but there was nothing I could actually pinpoint as heresy or even as unbiblical.

The angel said something which the prophet found difficult to believe. The prophet responded, "You'll have to show me where that one is in the Bible." The angel answered, "That's found in the Book of Daniel, chapter and verse such-and-such." This whole situation shocked me so much I don't remember the such-and-such. I had a Bible with me though. I opened it to the specific verse the angel had directed the prophet to. I read it. I had to read it again—not even close. It couldn't even be twisted to say what the angel had claimed. I looked up at the prophet. *He's lying*, I thought. At that very moment God spoke. It was unmistakable; not audible, but certainly clear. *Stand up and stop him!*

No! No, no, no, I begged. *God, please don't make me do this.*

My heart pounded. One of my legs shook uncontrollably. My mind raced.

Everyone in the room believes this guy. What's going to happen if I try to interrupt him?

The conflict between God's will and my fear raged the rest of the evening. I left the meeting that night having stayed quiet and in my seat the entire time.

Outside the church, in the falling snow, I couldn't help but think about what had happened. Not the 'false prophet' part, but the "I disobeyed God" part. I'm absolutely convinced that one day I will stand before God and hear him ask, *When I told you to stand up and stop him, why did you disobey me?*

And what will my answer be: *Seventy-five awestruck people in one room affect me more than you do*?

I bowed my head. *God, from now on I'll do whatever you ask me to do. I'll never disobey you again.*

From the night of that commitment, that rededication, to the very moment of this writing, I've heard God's voice and obeyed what he has said time and time again. I would categorize most of these experiences as simple and easy—like believing that "my relationships are based on a true caring for the person." But every once in awhile, a story unfolds. Like the time ...

Does it seem odd that someone would commit themselves to obeying God's voice?

... Outside the chapel, in the misty rain, I couldn't help but thank God for the miracle of the airline tickets and hotel reservation. *I wanted so much to be here at the funeral for Rosie's family.* I saw Rosie's daughter as I walked up the steps. God said to me, *Tell Cathy she'll smile again. ...*

Everything I've just shared was in my heart and mind as I listened to the atheist during his debate. He seemed very authentic in his doubt. If only he knew that 'relationship with God' actually means *friendship*, not *religion*. If only I could ask him, "What if it's not a 'standard set too unreasonably high for everyone'? Instead, what if it's an indication of what's possible in our lives as we experience our friendship with God?

"What if, because of God's influence, we actually *could* love 'all other human beings with the same strong, heart-felt desire to help, the same thought and compassion as we love ourselves'? What if this 'much higher demand' was certainly possible as we yielded ourselves to him?"

Didn't Jesus say that all things are possible with God[14]?

If it's possible, then in the words of our atheist friend, let's "try taking all this seriously."

8 Great Wonders is based on one thing and one thing only—the experience of a real relationship with God. I can say without hesitation that the Bible teaches that we can all experience complete fulfillment in a friendship with God. It's a fact, in black and white on the printed page. But I have no idea how the experiences will play out if you choose to begin this friendship.

I can also say confidently that the Bible teaches that God speaks to his people. Again, nothing gray about it. But I can't tell you the exact things he'll say to you as you develop your own relationship with him.

Despite my knowledge of the Bible, I have no clue what God will use next to challenge and reshape me, to deepen my friendship with him. All I know is that, whatever it is, he and I will go through it together.

Now that's a relationship, not a religion.

The Extra Effort (Search & Rescue)

⇚ Have you ever believed that God does not exist? Do you know someone who has considered themselves an atheist or an agnostic? What led you or your friend to this conclusion?

⇚ Who would you want on your debate team; an atheist or a Christian without a biblical worldview? Why? Who would you want praying for your sick child; a person without a biblical worldview or a person who hears from God? Why?

⇚ The author shared several stories in which he said God spoke to him. Do you think the author has schizophrenia? How comfortable are you with the idea of God speaking *personally* with you?

* * *

∜ If you can, note a recent news story, as well as a personal story, that relates to topics in this chapter.

News:

Personal:

∜ List two things that impacted you as you read the chapter or participated in a group discussion.

Scoring for *Search & Rescue* discussion groups:

Read-4 ∗ Notes-8 ∗ News-1 ∗ Personal-2 ∗ Impact-16 ∗ Total-_____

_____

[1] The atheist's statements are not directly quoted, but are a thought-by-thought paraphrase of comments made during the formal debate I attended.

[2] George Barna, quoted by Tim Stafford. "The Third Coming of George Barna," Christianity Today August 5th, 2002.

[3] www.Barna.org – We appreciate *The Barna Group* for granting permission for us to use their statistics in our book.

[4] The Barna Group, "Most Adults Feel Accepted by God, But Lack a Biblical Worldview" August 9th, 2005, June 14th, 2006 <http://www.barna.org/FlexPage.aspx?Page=BarnaUpdate&BarnaUpdateID=194>. (see also "A Biblical Worldview Has a Radical Effect on a Person's Life" December 1st, 2003, June 14th, 2006. <http://www.barna.org/FlexPage.aspx?Page=BarnaUpdate&BarnaUpdateID=154>.)

[5] Truth: Psalm 119:160, John 8:31-32, Ecclesiastes 12:9-14

[6] Bible Authority: 2 Timothy 3:16-17, Revelation 22:18-19, Deuteronomy 4:2-8

[7] Bible Accuracy: *historically*–Luke 1:1-4 & 3:1-6, *personally*–Hebrews 4:12

[8] Was Jesus sinless? Luke 23:39, 1 John 3:5, Hebrews 4:14-16

[9] Is salvation earned? Romans 6:23, Ephesians 2:8-9, Romans 4:1-8

[10] Sharing Religious Beliefs: Matthew 28:19-20, Acts 1:8, 2 Timothy 4:1-5

[11] A Personal Devil: Mark 1:12-13, John 8:44, 1 John 3:7-8

[12] God's Sovereign Authority: 1 Chronicles 29:11, Matthew 6:9-13, Romans 14:10-12

[13] Thomas S. Szasz, The Second Sin (New York: Anchor/Doubleday, 1973), 113.

[14] Matthew 19:26, Mark 10:27, Luke 18:27

[15] Start at the bottom right corner. Read diagonally, one character up and to the left. Wrap around the box of letters 76 times following this pattern, ending in the upper left corner.

2 ❧ What Could Have Been, Will Be

Relationship is intended.

Principles of a Wonderful Trip

DAD. *(Gathers his wife and children for a family meeting.)* We will be taking our annual vacation four months from today. My friend Jim[1] at work suggested that we might really enjoy Yellowstone National Park. What do you think?

FAMILY. *(Cheering in unison:)* Hooray!

(It's just a story.)

Principle #1:

Make the necessary arrangements with the destination in mind.

DAD. I told Jim that we could borrow Uncle Vincent's pop-up camper and drive to Yellowstone, but he says it's a two-day drive from here. We don't want to spend four days of our vacation on the road. *(To his wife:)* Sweetheart, since you're the computer guru I'm going to ask you to go online and make our reservations. We'll fly into Billings, Montana, and come in from the northeast. We need to book a cabin a couple of miles outside the park. And we also need to rent a hard-shell camper.

MOM. A hard-shell camper?

DAD. It will protect us from the bears.

(The children's eyes are as big as saucers.)

Principle #2:
Once reservations are set, adjust your priorities.

(The following morning, Mom goes over the airline itinerary and lets the family know that everything is confirmed.)

MOM. I can't wait for the trip. I called Aunt Maria last night and got some natural recipes to try while we're out in the wild.

DAD. Honey, don't forget that you're on vacation, too. Besides, every moment spent cooking is a moment not spent enjoying the great outdoors.

SON. Dad, I'm saving all my money for the trip. I have $13.37 so far.

DAD. That's great, son. We're all going to have to save our money. With airline fares, cabin and camper rentals, meals out, and park fees, this trip looks to cost around $3,000. There's going to be some changes in this family's spending habits for a while.

Principle #3:
Remember why you've made the changes you've made, and stay committed to your decision.

DAD. But, sweetheart, a Surround Sound System like this one has never been this cheap before. And the sale ends tomorrow.

MOM. It's only been two weeks, and you've already forgotten about Yellowstone? You know we can't afford the trip and a TV. You don't want to disappoint the children, do you?

DAD. You're right. And why did you have to bring the kids into it?

Principle #4:
Prepare for the destination. Then prepare some more.

> **DAD.** *(Asking for help from his friend:)* Jim, I was hoping you would look over my checklist to make sure I haven't left off anything important.
>
> **JIM.** Let's have a look-see. *(Mumbles through the list.)* Camera, good. Do you have any binoculars? *(Mumbles.)* Sleeping bags. Take some extra blankets. The nights are cold whatever time of year you go. *(Mumbles.)* New boots? If you've never been hiking before I would suggest trying out some of the trails around here first. You'll get a good feel for it. Plus, you'll break in your boots. *(Mumbles through the rest of the list.)* Don't forget insect repellant and sunscreen.
>
> **DAD.** Yikes, I'm glad I talked to you.
>
> **JIM.** I would also suggest visiting with a Park Ranger and picking up some trail maps before you hike. You can ask about things like building campfires, and he'll talk to you about do's and don'ts. Most people are unaware of the park's dangers.
>
> **DAD.** Dangers?
>
> **JIM.** Yeah, a lot of injuries in the park are buffalo-related. They're really kind of mean.

Principle #5:
To stay focused, 'see' the destination.

> **MOM.** Jim, we're so glad that you and Mary joined us for dinner. These last two months have been kind of tough on the kids. I was hoping you would share some stories from your past trips to Yellowstone.
>
> **JIM.** Glad to. The most wonderful place on earth is called the Grand Canyon of the Yellowstone. You've never seen a rainbow until you've seen one there in the spray from the waterfalls.
>
> **SON.** Mr. Lewis, I thought Old Faithful was the favorite sight in Yellowstone.
>
> **JIM.** The entire park is spectacular.
>
> **DAUGHTER.** Mrs. Lewis, what's your favorite sight there?
>
> **MARY.** I've never seen meadows as beautiful as they are in Yellowstone. Sounds a little silly to go to the mountains and

enjoy the meadows most, but they're just filled with elk and other kinds of wildlife.

Principle #6:
As the anticipation and excitement build, enjoy the experience.

MOM. Wake up, children. Today's the day.

* * *

Mission Statement

I once heard a speaker[2] say, "Your direction in life must determine your decisions, or else your decisions in life will certainly determine your direction." Are you employed in the area of your college major? Most graduates cannot answer yes. So, what happened? What could help us to become a voice of direction, rather than become a victim of decisions?

I have a limited amount of experience in the business world. I'm not an expert of experts, but here's something I do know. *To achieve success in any endeavor, you must have a mental snapshot of the desired outcome which has the strength to pull you through the realities of today.*

A few individuals I know, as well as almost every company I've heard of, have a mission statement. A mission statement is simply a word picture of the outcome one desires. For example, if you were in business to manufacture widgets, then your mission statement might read: *To put widgets in the hands of every family in the USA.*

Let's say the widget business is good, but to make it better your Board of Directors recommends that the company run television spots and they believe you should star in the commercials. You look at your mission statement and the answer is obvious. You say yes.

The buying public loves seeing your face and remembers the company's name. Noting your success, someone suggests that you should also endorse products and services for other companies; actually become an actor in TV ads. *That's cool,* you think. *Fame and fortune can be mine.*

But wait a minute. Your mission statement reads: *To put 'widgets' in the hands of every family in the USA.* If this future is going to take place, you really have no choice but to say no and stay focused on widgets. Right?

Would it surprise you to know that God has a mission statement? It's really not all that complex. It's a single phrase, made up of only four words: *The kingdom of God.*

'The kingdom of God' has been God's direction since the beginning. It has been the determining factor in all of his decisions from even before he said, "Let us make man in our image[3]." I believe that if we were to see God's home movies of the moment he spoke those words, and we looked closely at what's in the background of the shot, we would see that God was standing in front of his kingdom. After all, Jesus Christ told us that one day he will say, "Come, you who are blessed by my Father, inherit the kingdom that has been prepared for you since the foundation of the world.[4]" This means that the kingdom was prepared before Adam and Eve were created.

Our goal for this chapter is to see the connection between the first great wonder—*God Creates People*—and the last great wonder—*God and People, Together Forever.*

Do you already see it?

The connection will be seen more clearly if you're willing to do some homework. Within the next couple of days, I want you to read all four of these chapters; Genesis 1, Genesis 2, Revelation 21, and Revelation 22. Read them straight through as though they make up a single story. I've often referred to it as *The What-Could-Have-Been Bible.*

> Read *The What-Could-Have-Been Bible* in the next several days.

Here's what I've found in the story. The key thought in the first two chapters of the Bible says that God created mankind in his own image[5]. And the key thought in the last two chapters says that God will live with mankind, and they will be his people[6]. Genesis tells us that people were created to be *like* God. Revelation tells us that people are meant to be *with* God forever. It sounds to me as if God means for us to experience a relationship with him.

The Kingdom of God

I want to underline something we discussed a moment ago. _To achieve success in any endeavor, you must have a mental snapshot of the desired outcome which has the strength to pull you through the realities of today._ Keep in mind that a snapshot of the future by itself isn't enough. With the snapshot there must be a strong *pull* on our life, if there's going to be any lasting impact.

When Jesus spoke of the kingdom of God, he was certainly speaking in terms of a snapshot of the future. He mentioned that we would see Abraham, Isaac, Jacob, and all the prophets in the kingdom of God[7]. During the last supper, Jesus said, "I will never eat the Passover bread again, until it is fulfilled in the kingdom of God. I will not drink the fruit of the vine until the kingdom of God comes.[8]" But Jesus taught people about *the pull* of the kingdom more often than he spoke of the snapshot.

I want to take some of the things Jesus said about the kingdom of God, or the kingdom of heaven, and put them in the context of the *Principles of a Wonderful Trip*, which is where we began the chapter.

✳ ✳ ✳

Principle #1:

Make the necessary arrangements with the destination in mind.

- [15]... *"The time is fulfilled, and the kingdom of God is at hand; repent and believe in the gospel."*   Mark 1:15
- [3]... *"Truly I say to you, unless you are converted and become like children, you will not enter the kingdom of heaven."*   Matthew 18:3
- [3]... *"Truly, truly, I say to you, unless one is born again he cannot see the kingdom of God."*   John 3:3

Listen to the concepts behind these Bible words.

Repent—turn 180° and move in God's direction.

Believe in the gospel—buy into the message of God's mission.

Be converted—be changed.

Become like children—start fresh.

How is all of this possible? *Be born again*—God replaces the deadness we find inside us with his kind of life.

Remember, if we never purchase tickets for our vacation getaway, all we will ever experience is the travel brochure.

Principle #2:

Once reservations are set, adjust your priorities.

- [33]*"But seek first his kingdom and his righteousness, and all these things* [food, water and clothing] *will be added to you."*   Matthew 6:33
- [29]... *"Truly I say to you, there is no one who has left house or wife or brothers or parents or children, for the sake of the kingdom of God,* [30]*who will not receive many times as much at this time and in the age to come, eternal life."*   Luke 18:29-30

Look at the deal God offers: *Make the priorities of my kingdom your top priority, and I'll make the priorities of your life my top priority.* In essence, he's asking us to adopt his mission statement as our own. It's simple, but not easy. And we'll never buy into making this adjustment until we believe it's worth it. Jesus spoke like it is.

Principle #3:
Remember why you've made the changes you've made, and stay committed to your decision.

- [62]... *"No one, after putting his hand to the plow and looking back, is fit for the kingdom of God."*
  Luke 9:62

But interestingly ...

- [32]*"Do not be afraid, little flock, for your Father has chosen gladly to give you the kingdom."*
  Luke 12:32

The destination is established and our priorities are outlined. But afterwards, we only manage to muster a half-commitment. And I'm not even talking about Christianity! We're less-than-committed in our jobs, in our friendships, in life in general. It's human nature. So Jesus addressed our human nature with a very harsh statement: *Anything less than 100% commitment is unacceptable.* But then, he also reminded us that this whole kingdom idea is based on God's generosity and his love for us.

Principle #4:
Prepare for the destination. Then prepare some more.

- [11]... *"To you it has been granted to know the mysteries of the kingdom of heaven."*
  Matthew 13:11
- [21]*"Not everyone who says to me, 'Lord, Lord,' will enter the kingdom of heaven, but he who does the will of my Father who is in heaven will enter."*
  Matthew 7:21
- [52]... *"Therefore every scribe who has become a disciple of the kingdom of heaven is like a head of a household, who brings out of his treasure things new and old."*
  Matthew 13:52

Let's say we're in Paris and we only speak English. Is it more realistic to expect Parisians to stop speaking French around us, or to find an interpreter?

Welcome to Kingdom Speak 101. Since knowing the local language of our destination increases our participation and enjoyment of the local culture, let's begin learning the language of the kingdom. The following is a list of phrases spoken by Jesus. I call them *Jesus Verbs*:

Follow me, believe me, practice truth, worship, celebrate and rejoice,
let your light shine, freely give, love me, keep my word, pray and fast,
ask, seek, knock, take courage, come to me, hear my words,
act on them, forgive, take up your cross, humble yourself,
hear my voice, serve others, count the cost, praise God,
keep watching and praying, receive the Holy Spirit, shepherd my sheep,
go, preach, make disciples, baptize them, teach them.

Experiencing the customs and culture of the kingdom prepares us for life in the kingdom. And our embracing of the *Jesus Verbs* will quite naturally be accompanied by the pull of the kingdom in our life.

Principle #5:
   To stay focused, 'see' the destination.

- *3"Blessed are the poor in spirit, for theirs is the kingdom of heaven."*

   Matthew 5:3
- *10"Blessed are those who have been persecuted for the sake of righteousness, for theirs is the kingdom of heaven."*   *Matthew 5:10*

When we experience a change of heart for the better, we're later tempted to change our mind. Initial decisions are followed by internal doubt. Likewise, the pull of the kingdom in our life, even over the long haul, will be challenged by the push to keep us down.

What is it that will help us overcome the weight on our shoulders?

It's been my experience that the stories and fellowship of others who are on the same path provide the greatest encouragement to keep moving forward. That's when I see the destination all over again. That's when I feel the blessing of kingdom life.

Principle #6:
   As the anticipation and excitement build, enjoy the experience.

Here's the amazing thing about the trip. It's different for all of us. I intentionally skipped over scriptures for this principle because your own journey will be completely unique and different from anyone else's. For this principle, I don't want us to focus on biblical commonality, but rather, on a personal friendship with God.

And let me say this: Even though the trip is personal, you don't have to keep it to yourself. It's okay to tell others about it. It's okay to take others with us.

You know, it's likely that someone will ask us how we can believe in a kingdom no one has ever seen. But if we've seen *the pull* of the kingdom in the lives of other people and it has strengthened the pull in our own lives, then it's not difficult to believe at all.

*   *   *

The Pull in One Man's Life[9]

The late Charlie Ragus had a huge impact on my life. Most of what I've learned about personal development and leadership I learned through my association with one of the companies he founded. I believe that, through his influence, he helped prepare me for the work I now do as a writer and teacher.

Charlie was a wonderful storyteller. The last time I saw him, he held a Bible in his hand as he shared a wonderful story of the pull in his life.

Charlie told two of his close associates, Rick and Brian, that he wanted them to join him on an important visit to a friend they all knew. The purpose, he said simply, was to share the message of Jesus Christ with this man.

Charlie grabbed his Bible as the three men left to see their friend. They flew to an unattended airstrip near a mountain where the man lived. When they got off the plane they stood together holding hands, praying for the rest of their journey and for God's work to be completed in their friend's heart. Then they drove up the mountain to their friend's home.

What would compel Charlie to go to such great lengths; a plane trip, a drive up a mountain? What could make someone feel such a sense of purpose?

Rick shared with me later that "When we arrived, Charlie wasted no time in going to the heart of the matter. He walked our friend through the *Romans Road*[10], and led him in a prayer of commitment."

I hear Rick's words and can picture the hugs and moist eyes.

Charlie then joked that since Rick was an ordained minister, he was obviously the one meant to baptize their friend in the frigid waters of a nearby river. Rick recalled with a smile that "the water in the river was only about 20 inches deep, and was around 35 degrees ... it was a quick baptism." But what a moment it must have been.

I'm sure that as this dear friend felt the pull of the river near his home, that Charlie felt a fresh pull on his heart from the kingdom of God.

And it may seem like a stretch, but I can imagine God and Adam, just after Creation, sitting on the bank of another river, the river that flowed from the Garden of Eden[11]. As they watch sunlight glimmer on the water, God's thoughts wander—from a river which will begin at his throne in the kingdom[12], to the icy waters that rush down the side of a mountain near the home of Charlie's friend.

Adam sees the far-away look in God's eyes. "Lord, what are you thinking about?"

He smiles. "I was thinking about how beautiful the river is."

The Extra Effort (Search & Rescue)

❧ Let's say that life is a trip. Which of the *Principles of a Wonderful Trip* do you feel you might need to address next in your life? How are you progressing up the highway towards your destination?

_____

_____

_____

❧ How do you respond to *purpose* and *goals*? What kind of future could pull you through today's hardships? How willing are you to adopt the mission statement, "created to be like God, meant to be with God," as your own?

_____

_____

_____

❧ Read through the list of *Jesus Verbs* near the top of page 20. How much of this "language of the kingdom" are you currently *doing*? Underline three verbs you are already doing, and (circle) three verbs you could start soon.

....

....

....

* * *

❧ If you can, note a recent news story, as well as a personal story, that relates to topics in this chapter.

........News:...

........Personal:..

❧ List two things that impacted you as you read the chapter or participated in a group discussion.

....

....

....

Scoring for *Search & Rescue* discussion groups:
  *Read-4 * Notes-8 * News-1 * Personal-2 * Impact-16 * Total-_____*

[1] In the family vacation to Yellowstone story, the character of Jim is based on my friend and ministry partner Brian. I am the Dad character, who knows virtually nothing about camping. Thanks for the 411, Brian.

[2] John Crudele, CSP / www.JohnCrudele.com

[3] Genesis 1:26

[4] Matthew 25:34

[5] Genesis 1:27

[6] Revelation 21:3

[7] Luke 13:28

[8] Luke 22:16, 18

[9] Special thanks to Rick Loy (the minister who baptized his friend and Charlie's) for refreshing my memory and filling in gaps in the story.

[10] The *Romans Road* is a series of scriptures which have led many to receive God's salvation. I noted the following version in my Bible when I was in high school: First, Romans 3:10, then Romans 3:23, Romans 5:12, Romans 6:23, Revelation 20:14-15, Romans 5:8, Romans 10:13, and 1 John 5:11-13.

[11] Genesis 2:10

[12] Revelation 22:1

What Could Have Been, Will Be

3 ❧ Separated, Condemned, Executed

Salvation is necessary.

What If?

The serpent was the craftiest animal that the Lord God made. One day it said to Eve, "C'mon, has God really said that you cannot eat from any tree in the garden?"

The woman answered, "Sure, we can eat fruit from the trees in the garden, but about the tree that is in the middle of the garden, God did say, 'You cannot eat from it or even touch it, or you will die.'"

The serpent said to the woman, "You will not die! Listen, God knows that the day you eat from it your eyes will be opened, and you will be just like him, knowing good and evil."

*The woman saw that the tree produced good food, that it was beautiful to look at, and that it could make her wise[1] ... **but she told the serpent no**.*

The man and his wife heard the sound of the Lord God walking in the garden in the cool of the day[2], and they ran to be with him.

What if, in that most decisive moment in human history, the decision had been made to resist the temptation and to obey God?

If that were the case, then Cain wouldn't have murdered Abel. God wouldn't have destroyed the world with a flood. Sodom and Gomorrah would have remained to this day as cities of righteousness rather than bywords of wretchedness.

Between the first two chapters in the Bible, which tell of God's Creation, and the last two, which tell of his kingdom, there are 1,185 chapters. As though situated between parentheses, they tell of the catastrophe of sin and its solution. But if there was no sin that separates, then there would be no Law that condemns and no Crucifixion. No need. These chapters in the Bible would be gone.

It's not just Bible events that would be affected. Many events of secular history would also be erased. There would be no *Trojan Horse*, no Alexander the Great, no *Ides of March*. There would be no *Holy War*, no Genghis Khan, no *Black Death*, and no Conquistadores. There would be no Ivan the Terrible, no Calcutta's 'Black Hole,' no Zulu's 'Blood River.' There would be no *American Civil War*, no *Battle of Little Bighorn*. There would be no *Bloody Sunday*, no *War to End War*, no Bolsheviks. There would be no Hitler, no *Holocaust*, no *Pearl Harbor*, and no *Hiroshima*. There would be no terrorist attacks on September 11th, 2001.

And what about our own personal histories? Think about this for a moment; no pain we've caused, no heartaches we've experienced. No skeletons in the closet, no bondages, no fear. Right now we would be experiencing peace and tranquility in God's kingdom, where lions lay down with lambs. God's face would be the first thing we saw this morning. His voice, the last thing we hear before we sleep at night.

Of course, all of this is difficult ... well, all of this is impossible to imagine because Eve didn't say no. She and Adam didn't run to be with God.

* * *

Crime and Punishment

At two minutes after nine, on the morning of April 19th, 1995, a bomb destroyed the Alfred P. Murrah Federal Building in Oklahoma City, Oklahoma. About 90 minutes later, Timothy McVeigh was arrested on a firearms charge during a routine traffic stop. Two days later, only hours before he was expected to make bail on the weapons charge, Federal authorities arrested McVeigh in connection with the explosion that killed 168 people, including 19 children. Less than four months later, a Federal grand jury indicted McVeigh (along with Terry Nichols) on murder and conspiracy charges.

With arrest and indictment, McVeigh was *separated* from the society against which he had committed his crimes.

McVeigh's trial took place about two years after his arrest. The amount of evidence brought against him was absolutely staggering. The trial lasted two months and resulted in McVeigh being convicted on all 11 murder and conspiracy counts against him. On June 13th, 1997 the jury condemned McVeigh to die, and on August 14th he was formally sentenced to death.

With conviction and sentencing, McVeigh was *condemned* to die by the laws of the society against which he had committed his crimes.

McVeigh argued that since the government claimed his victims were "not just the dead but America itself," then the country should be allowed to witness his punishment. "I am going to demand they televise it nationally," he said. That did not happen. On June 21st, 2001 McVeigh died by lethal injection. McVeigh's last statement is said to be from the poem *Invictus*[3] by William Ernest Henley (1849-1903).

> *It matters not how strait the gate,*
> *How charged with punishments the scroll,*
> *I am the master of my fate:*
> *I am the captain of my soul.*

When McVeigh was *executed*, the penalty was paid in full and justice was granted to the society against which he had committed his crimes.

✳ ✳ ✳

We Have a Problem

Wow. And the *8 Great Wonders* started out so positively. We've talked about a relationship with God—how it's possible to experience relational dynamics with him, like conversation. And we began by talking about how this relationship is revealed through God's history with people—the *8 Great Wonders*. In the last chapter we looked at the connection between the first great wonder and the eighth, and we saw a future kingdom that can have a positive pull in our lives today. Now, suddenly, we're talking about crime and punishment, sin and its consequence. Especially its consequence.

The Bible refers to us, before we've accepted God's salvation, as people who are dead. We're dead in our trespasses and sins[4]. We're alienated, or excluded, from the life of God[5]. The Bible says that the gospel is preached to those who are dead[6].

If I could offer evidence which would show this to be true, I would ask our atheist friend from Chapter 1 to stand here beside me. I'm sure he would tell us that he has never, in any way, experienced God in his life. He might tell us that he has never seen God, heard God, smelled, tasted, or touched God. He could tell us in all sincerity that he has drawn a conclusion; that the lack of sensory evidence is one of the proofs that there is no God.

The interesting thing about this is that the Bible is in agreement with our friend when he says he hasn't experienced God. But the Bible offers a different reason. It isn't because God does not exist. It's because that part of us which was created in the image of God, created to be like God, is dead.

And death is a consequence.

We're about to see in this chapter that our death before God is the connection between the second, third, and fourth great wonders: *People Sin Against God*, *God's Law Is Given*, and *Jesus Christ Dies*.

The Death Process

To really see this connection, we're going to look at three specific Bible verses from the Book of Romans; a mini-Bible study if you will.

The Book of Romans is actually a letter written by a man named Paul to the Christians who lived in Rome. Paul was an Apostle of Jesus Christ, although he didn't believe in Jesus when the Christian church began. He hated Christianity and persecuted its first believers. But Jesus revealed himself to Paul in an astounding way, and turned him around 180°. Paul became a great influence in the Christian church, and he uses his letter to the Romans as an opportunity to help people understand God's plan for us.

He begins by saying that we can certainly know there is a God, because of what we see in nature[7]. But he admits that we wouldn't know this by looking at human nature[8]. We've fallen dramatically short of the lives we're meant to live[9]. We are sinners who need a savior. Paul explains to the Christians in Rome, and to us as well, that we're dead. And he tells us when it happened.

First, we were all separated from God because of Adam's sin.

> [12]*... through one man [Adam] sin entered into the world, and death through sin, and so death spread to all men, ...*
>
> *Romans 5:12*

We can ask any number of knowledgeable Christians what the word *death* means in this verse, and we'll hear a consistent answer: *Death is separation from God.* Part of the punishment for Adam and Eve's disobedience was being kicked out of the Garden of Eden[10]. Worse than that, God also removed his presence, as they had known it, from the earth. They had walked and talked with him side-by-side. And I'm sure we would all agree—we have no clue what that might have been like, having never experienced anything close to it.

Death *is* separation from God, but that's not the end of it. Paul went on to say that death reigned from Adam to Moses, even over people who didn't commit Adam's sin[11]. He specifically said "from Adam to Moses." He also said that sin isn't judged when there is no law[12]. References to Moses and the Law lead to the second verse I want us to consider:

> [9]*I was once alive apart from the Law; but when the commandment came, sin became alive and I died;*　　　*Romans 7:9*

Then the Law condemned every one of us to die as sinners.

"When the commandment came ... I died?"

This verse comes only 41 verses after the previous one we looked at, Romans 5:12. "Through Adam ... death spread to all men."

Keep in mind that we aren't pulling scriptures from just anywhere in the Bible. These verses are from the same letter by the same writer to the same people.

Is this the same death? Did God's Law condemn us to a death we already experienced in Adam? No. The Law didn't sentence us to be separated. It doomed us to be destroyed. It may be surprising to learn that each of the Ten Commandments can be found elsewhere in the Bible with a death penalty clause. We'll explore this in detail in a later chapter.

Many people hold on to God's Law like it's a rulebook for life. We believe that the Law will shape our personal morality, but we often see a different result in the lives of those who hold on the tightest. Time and again, we find people who have become paralyzed by guilt and shame. Or we find judgmental people who have become filled with self-righteousness. This happens because God's Law doesn't have the effect of a rulebook on us, but rather, the effect of a courtroom. The Law condemns us all to die as sinners, and it's this death that we find in the final verse from Romans that we'll take a look at.

> [6]*... our old self was crucified with [Christ], ...*　　　*Romans 6:6*

Finally, we were crucified with Christ, which is why we must be born again.

So in light of these three scriptures, here's the big question. At what point did we die?

A. In Adam—*through one man*
B. Through the Law—*when the commandment came*
C. With Christ
    Or maybe:
D. All of the above

I remember my reaction when I first heard that someone had been arrested in the Oklahoma City bombing. I thought, *If the Federal Government thinks it has a case against this guy, he's a dead man.* Was Timothy McVeigh dead while he was jailed? No. But he was as good as dead. He was on the path and there was no turning back … just like it was for the whole human race; 'jailed' and separated from God once Adam sinned.

When I heard that the prosecution against McVeigh had evidence which included more than 10,000 pages of documents[13], I was stunned. *This guy is absolutely dead. They're going to bury him six 'hundred' feet under ground.* So when the jury condemned him, was he dead? Not yet. But death was coming. It was inevitable … just like it was for all of us sinners after our 'trial and conviction,' when Moses brought the stone tablets off the mountain.

I was sitting in my car, listening to news coverage of McVeigh's execution on the radio. And I remember the announcement that he was finally dead.

Paul makes an announcement in the Bible. "The love of God compels me to preach," he says, "because I am convinced that if Jesus Christ died for everybody,"—here's the announcement—"everybody died."[14] This is why we're not born into this world already experiencing a relationship with God. It doesn't happen automatically. In clear terms, here's why people *must* be born again. When Jesus died for us, we died with him.

Convinced and Compelled

Now, I don't know *how* we died with Christ, but I do understand the effect this belief had on Paul. He was 'convinced' and 'compelled.'

Paul traveled thousands of miles preaching the message of salvation through Jesus in cities where no one had ever heard it before[15]. Take a look at *Paul's Missionary Journeys* in the section of maps that can be found in many Bibles. He endured terrible hardships during his travels, saying they were proof that he was a servant of Christ[16]. Paul wrote:

24Five times I received from the Jews thirty-nine lashes. 25Three times I was beaten with rods, once I was stoned, three times I was shipwrecked, a night and a day I have spent in the deep. 26I have been on frequent journeys, in dangers from rivers, dangers from robbers, dangers from my countrymen, dangers from the Gentiles, dangers in the city, dangers in the wilderness, dangers on the sea, dangers among false brethren; 27I have been in labor and hardship, through many sleepless nights, in hunger and thirst, often without food, in cold and exposure. 28Apart from such external things, there is the daily pressure on me of concern for all the churches.
                                                                        2 Corinthians 11:24-28

After the first hardship, I think most of us would have been questioning whether this was really the ministry God wanted for us.

Much of Paul's second letter to the Corinthian church was written with ministry in mind. He raised the idea of ministry in a general sense in Chapter 3. He made it personal in Chapter 4 when he wrote, "Since we have this ministry ... we do not lose heart" (4:1). "We are afflicted in every way, but not crushed; perplexed, but not despairing; persecuted, but not forsaken; struck down, but not destroyed; always carrying about in the body the dying of Jesus, so that the life of Jesus also may be manifested in our body" (4:8-10). In Chapter 5, Paul addressed the accusation that he must be crazy for doing what he was doing. "If we are beside ourselves, it is for God; if we are of sound mind, it is for you" (5:13).

The Apostle Paul endured the hardships he endured, accomplishing the mission he accomplished, because he believed the truth he believed. Convinced we died with Christ, he was compelled by God's love to reach us with the gospel.

In the very next breath, Paul tells us why he did what he did and endured what he endured. It was because of what he believed.

14For the love of Christ controls us, having concluded this, that one died for all, therefore all died;
                                                                        2 Corinthians 5:14

This verse is one of eight verses in the New Testament which associates our death directly with Christ's death for us. I believe that when Jesus died for us, we died *spiritually* with him. And that means we have an immediate issue to deal with. It's not just that one day in the future we'll stand before God and be judged, with a possibility of being damned to a lake that burns with fire and brimstone. That's true, but the Bible refers to that outcome as "the Second Death[17]." Our immediate issue is that we've already experienced the first death. We've already been separated, condemned and executed. And unless we're born again, we will not see the kingdom of God[18].

When I understood this truth, it changed everything for me. I didn't think any more in terms of: *When I'm lonely I need Jesus the Friend. When I'm sick I need Jesus the Healer. The poor need Jesus the Provider. The addicted need Jesus the Liberator.* I realized that these conditions may be symptoms of a bigger root cause.

Dead people need life. Live people need relationship. All people need Jesus—period.

NOTES

What Do These Two People Need?

Scott was a really decent guy. He was a hard worker and a good friend. He loved his children. He cared deeply for his wife. The way he lived his life, I would have thought that Scott was a Christian. He did have a church background, but he wasn't attending church at this time in his life. He had questions about things he didn't understand, and I was doing my best to give him some food for thought.

Judy, on the other hand, attended church faithfully. She had been a member of a good church for quite a number of years, and had experienced the best that church life has to offer. But Judy had grown bitter and angry and took it out on anyone who was nearby.

Judy and I worked in a mailroom. I remember one day sitting there together. We were focused on our jobs and had been silent for awhile. Out of nowhere Judy started ranting and raving at God. She was looking at me, but yelling at him. When she calmed down for a moment, I responded, "Judy, all I said was good morning." She laughed, and the moment was wide-open for us to talk about some pretty tough issues.

I had been talking with Judy and Scott individually for several weeks when I realized something significant. I didn't know whether either one of them was really a Christian. I began praying, *Holy Spirit, show me what these two people need.* And I sensed that the answer came from this question: Has anything ever been said that indicates a personal friendship with God?

I thought about Scott first. He had a church background and was a decent person, but he had never said anything that indicated that God was working in his life, or that God had ever spoken to him. He had never talked in those terms. I sensed the Holy Spirit saying, *You need to share the gospel with Scott for the first time in his life.* A week later, a friend and I met with Scott over lunch. I shared the gospel with him, and he realized his need to be born again to begin his friendship with God. We had the privilege of praying with him as he accepted Jesus as his Savior and Lord. Scott began to grow as a Christian after that.

I also thought about the same question in regard to Judy. Had she ever said anything that indicated a personal friendship with God? And quite honestly, she had. She had shared a story with me.

In essence, one of her daughters was involved in a harmful lifestyle. The Holy Spirit had directed Judy to write a firm but loving letter to her daughter. She did exactly that, thinking the letter would impact her daughter, that her daughter would turn away from her lifestyle, and that mother and daughter would be closer than they had ever been before. Unfortunately, just the opposite happened. Judy's daughter decided to stop communicating, and Judy was angry about it. In her eyes, God was responsible for the broken relationship. God was mean, and he didn't really care about her.

The fact that Judy had been directed by the Holy Spirit showed me that she really did have a friendship with God. Her issues had more to do with wrong perceptions of her heavenly Father and the relationship they shared.

I gave her a copy of *Classic Christianity*[19], a book which had changed my life. She read the book and was also impacted. One day, I was sitting in an office surrounded by other employees. All of the sudden, Judy flew around the corner, shouting with joy, "Eric, I've been worshipping the wrong God! He loves me and I understand that now!" Part of me wanted to crawl under the desk from embarrassment, but the better part of me wanted to shout *hallelujah* from the rooftop with her.

Here's the lesson I learned from my experiences with Scott and Judy. The question of 'relationship' is what reveals our greatest need. You know, if I had focused on Scott's goodness and decency, I don't know that he would have ever come to faith in Christ. If I had focused on Judy's bitterness and anger, and tried to 'save' her again, I doubt that she would have ever returned to the loving Father she had known in her earlier years.

The Extra Effort (Search & Rescue)

❧ Is the world that we live in the same as the world that God created? Why or why not? Are the people that God created the people we are? Explain your reasoning.

❧ What have you heard Christians say is a non-Christian's "great need"? How does this chapter's teaching that "we are dead" support or challenge that idea?

❧ Paul *endured* while he *accomplished* because he *believed*. What examples from Paul's life do you think might help us increase our endurance, accomplishment, and belief?

---

* * *

❧ If you can, note a recent news story, as well as a personal story, that relates to topics in this chapter.

News:

Personal:

❧ List two things that impacted you as you read the chapter or participated in a group discussion.

Scoring for *Search & Rescue* discussion groups:

*Read-4 * Notes-8 * News-1 * Personal-2 * Impact-16 * Total-_____*

1 *"The serpent was the craftiest animal ... that it could make her wise"*: This is based on Genesis 3:1-6a.

2 Genesis 3:8a

3 William Ernest Henley's poem, "Invictus," is in the public domain.

4 Ephesians 2:1

5 Ephesians 4:18

6 1 Peter 4:6

7 Romans 1:18-20

8 Romans 1:21-32

9 Romans 3:23

10 Genesis 3:24

11 Romans 5:14

12 Romans 5:13

13 I have since found a press release entitled "Attorney General Statement Regarding Timothy McVeigh," dated May 24th, 2001, which reads, in-part: "This particular investigation produced millions of records, including millions of pages of hotel, motel or phone records, over 238,000 photographs, over 28,000 reports of interviews and more than 23,000 pieces of evidence."

14 2 Corinthians 5:14

15 Romans 15:20

16 2 Corinthians 11:23

17 Revelation 20:14-15

18 John 3:3

19 Bob George, <u>Classic Christianity: Life's Too Short to Miss the Real Thing</u> (Eugene: Harvest House, 1989).

Separated, Condemned, Executed

4 ❧ Death = Death, Life = Life

Salvation is provided.

Jesus Christ is the central figure in Christianity. And right in the middle of the *8 Great Wonders* is the fourth wonder—*Jesus Christ Dies*—and the fifth wonder—*Jesus, Alive Again!*

I can imagine Jesus standing between these two headlines. With one foot in front of the cross he points towards the first three wonders, and says, "I died for you because you were created to be God's friend, but sin separated you from him. I died for you because the Law condemned you to die." Then, with the other foot in front of the empty tomb, he points in the direction of the last three wonders, saying, "I rose from the dead so that you can be born again, so that you can live by faith in the power of the Holy Spirit. I rose from the dead because you are meant to be with God forever."

The goal of this chapter is to present the connection between the fourth and fifth great wonders without lulling us all into a sense of 'been there, done that.' After all, the stories of Jesus' death and resurrection have been told millions of times; from Easter Sunday services, to passion plays and Hollywood movies. (The first motion picture featuring a portrayal of Jesus was made in 1897.)

We're going to see the connection between these events, arguably the greatest of the great wonders, from a logical, practical perspective. And this is where things get risky. Some have adopted a mentality about the death and resurrection of Jesus that says "we don't have to understand, we just have to believe." But we're going to take the risk. And maybe by looking at *how* we can have a relationship with God, we'll be moved emotionally by the reason *why* we can have this relationship.

*   *   *

The Most Offensive Words Ever Spoken

It's one thing to be controversial; it's quite another to be offensive. Statements made by Jesus qualify for both categories.

The night before he was crucified, Jesus had an interesting conversation[1] with his Apostles. He spent time trying to prepare them for what would take place later that night, into the next day, and beyond. Jesus told them that he would be leaving to prepare a place for them in his Father's house. He said that he would also be coming back for them so that they could be with him. Controversy surrounds statements like this.

Jesus continued by telling the men, "You know the way to get there."

One of them responded, "We don't even know where you are going. How do we know the way to get there?"

Many of us may be familiar with Jesus' answer. "I am the way, the truth, and the life," he said. "No one comes to the Father, except through me."

Jesus claimed to be the only way to God. For some people, these words are some of the most offensive ever spoken. "How can Jesus Christ be the *only* way? There are many world religions, many ways to get to God. After all, don't all religions teach the same thing basically?"

What Was Jesus' Claim Based On?

I can certainly understand why Jesus' words rub people the wrong way. Jesus was a teacher, just like many others. His lessons and parables are well-known, even to those among us who wouldn't consider themselves to be his followers. Many people are familiar with sayings of Jesus; like "turn the other cheek[2]" and "judge not, that you be not judged[3]." When people are called on to recite The Lord's Prayer[4] together, it always amazes me that even the most irreligious people join right in. Many people would raise their hand if asked, "Who knows the story of *Jesus Feeds Five Thousand*[5], or *The Parable of the Good Samaritan*[6], or *The Parable of the Prodigal Son*[7]?" And for those of us who watch sports on television, we're probably familiar with a placard that reads

'John 3:16.' This refers to the most well-known words Jesus ever spoke: "For God so loved the world, that he gave his only begotten Son, that whosoever believeth in him should not perish, but have everlasting life."

Non-Christians even go as far as to say that Jesus was a *great* teacher. They recognize that his teachings have influenced the world for 2,000 years. But let's be honest. He wasn't the only great teacher to affect the human race. Here are a few other influential ones.

- Siddhartha Gautama (The Buddha)—*Indian philosopher and founder of Buddhism*
- Confucius—*Chinese philosopher*
- Socrates—*Greek philosopher*
- Plato—*Greek philosopher*
- Aristotle—*Greek philosopher*
- Muhammad—*Arab prophet and founder of Islam*

This is by no means a comprehensive list. Even in contemporary times, we've learned lessons of passive resistance and civil rights from the Mahatma Gandhi and Martin Luther King, Jr.

However, when it comes to Jesus Christ, we need to understand that he did not make his claim to be the only way to God based on his great teaching ability or even on the lessons he taught. He made his claim based on two other abilities: his ability to be a sinless sacrifice on behalf of all humanity, and his ability to give all humanity the salvation we so desperately need.

In this chapter, we aren't going to compare Jesus to the other moral teachers. We're simply going to look at the answers to two questions.

1. Was Jesus qualified to die for *our* sins, rather than his own?
2. Did Jesus ever demonstrate that he had the ability to give us the salvation we need?

If the answer to either of these questions is no, then Christianity completely unravels.

"Was Jesus qualified to die for *our* sins, rather than his own?"

In the 1980s there was a movie called *The Last Temptation of Christ*. This controversial story depicts Jesus being tempted with thoughts of giving up on God's plan and embracing a normal life with a wife and family. I'm sure the idea was to show Jesus as someone who was just like us. However, we already know from the Bible that Jesus was tempted in every way that we are, yet without sin[8].

"Time out! Eric, didn't we discover from our mini-Bible study in the last chapter that, because of Adam, 'sin and death spread to all men'? How is it possible that Jesus was exempt from this truth?"

That's a good question. It makes sense that if Adam's sin and death spread to all people, then they were passed to Cain and Abel, and the rest of Adam's children. A contaminated Noah passed sin and death to his three sons, who were also saved by the ark. And a contaminated Abraham ...

Open a Bible to the Gospel of Matthew, Chapter 1, verses 2 through 16.

Actually, let's open the Bible to the first verses in the first book of the New Testament—the Gospel of Matthew. (Go ahead and really do this.) Let's follow the entire list of fathers and sons presented there, starting with verse two, and say, "*this father* (Abraham) passed sin and death to *this son* (Isaac), and *this father* (Isaac) passed sin and death to *this son* (Jacob)"—over and over.

Our statement would be true for 40 generations, but then, at the end of the list, the wording changes with a man named Joseph. Look at verse 16. *Joseph [was] the husband of Mary, by whom Jesus was born.* We discover the reason for the change in wording as we read the story of the baby Jesus in the rest of the chapter[9].

Somehow we started out with a question that has Good Friday/Easter implications: *Was Jesus qualified to die for our sins?* And now we find ourselves in the Christmas story. *Jesus was born of a virgin.*

If the medical experts of his day were able to run a paternity blood test on Jesus, what would they have discovered? They would have found that Jesus did not have Joseph's blood running through his veins. He did not have his mother Mary's blood running through his veins either.

From the book *The Chemistry of the Blood* by M. R. DeHaan, M.D.[10]:

The mother provides the fetus (the unborn developing infant) with the nutritive elements for the building of that little body in the secret of her womb, but all the blood which forms in it is formed in the embryo itself. From the time of conception to the time of birth of the infant not one single drop of blood ever passes from mother to child. The placenta, that mass of temporary tissue known better as "afterbirth," forming the link between mother and child, is so constructed that although all the soluble nutritive elements such as proteins, fats, carbohydrates, salts, minerals and even antibodies pass freely from mother to child and the waste products of the child's metabolism are passed back to the mother's circulation, no actual interchange of a single drop of blood ever occurs normally. All the blood which is in that child is produced within the child itself.

The Bible makes a big deal about the blood of Jesus. It says that we've been justified[11], we have redemption[12], and we've been purchased with his blood[13]. It says that the blood of Jesus cleanses us from all sin[14]. Someone may respond, "That all sounds like cryptic, symbolic Bible language. Weren't we going to talk in logical and practical terms?"

Buckle up.

The writer of the New Testament Book of Hebrews (a letter to the Jewish people) compares Jesus' death for our sins with the system of animal sacrifices[15] that we see clearly and tragically in the Old Testament. He says that the blood of bulls and goats only "covered over" previously committed sins, but that the blood of Jesus completely "takes away" all sins … for all time. He reminds his Jewish readers that the high priest went into the Most Holy Place one time a year to offer blood on behalf of the people, but that Jesus went directly into the presence of God in heaven one time in history to offer his blood for everyone. The writer tells us that the Old Testament sacrificial system was "copies of the things in the heavens" but that Jesus' death was "the heavenly things themselves."

The sacrificing of animals really is cruel and tragic. But I believe God wanted us to feel the heart-wrenching emotion of an innocent dying for the guilty. I don't think we were supposed to grow calloused towards it. If we can feel the unfairness of the 'copy,' maybe we can begin to see the horrific significance of Jesus' sacrifice for the sin in *our* lives. If we could even scratch the surface of 'the innocent dying for the guilty,' maybe, just maybe, we could begin to understand the great love that God has for us.

"For God so loved the world, that he gave his only begotten Son …"

Jesus really was qualified to be the sinless sacrifice for all sinners because he was the only begotten—which means *physically fathered*—Son of God. Can you see it? He was exempt from Adam's sin and death because he wasn't fathered by a descendant of Adam, but by God. He literally had God's blood running through his veins.

The *Why* Behind the *How*

NOTES

Hopefully, we understand that Christianity isn't based on things that we have to pretend are true. Hopefully, the *how* of how a relationship with God is possible makes sense to us. But then again, it's really not about the how. It's about the *why*.

If I could, I would develop a new kind of paper to print the *8 Great Wonders* message on. What would be different about the new paper is this: It would hold the words that express God's plan for our salvation only until the reader 'gets it,' only until it all clicks. Then the plan would disappear from the pages, and all that would be left would be the motivation behind the plan. All that would remain would be the grace of God.

Grace is intense; like someone's attempt to rescue a baby who is buried alive.

Grace is God's love. Not a romantic daydreaming kind of love; God's grace is extreme love in action. I can't imagine a greater definition for grace than this: "For God so loved the world, that he gave his only begotten Son, that whosoever believeth in him should not perish, but have everlasting life." And I can't imagine a greater demonstration of God's grace for us either.

Notice that the verse doesn't say *for God so loved the plan*. The message of the gospel isn't about the plan as much as it's about the love that God feels in his heart for us. And the very day Jesus died for us, something wonderful happened in God's heart.

Take a look at 2 Corinthians 5:19, which begins "God was in Christ, reconciling the world to himself." In the last chapter we saw a death process which began when Adam and Eve disobeyed God. With sin came separation from God. But separation is reversed by reconciliation. In Christ, God ended the world's separation from himself.

The verse goes on to say that God is "no longer holding our sins against us"—a great definition of forgiveness. The second part of the death process was condemnation. We were condemned by the Law to die as sinners. But condemnation is nullified by forgiveness. In Christ, God let go of the condemnation hanging over our lives.

The word *gospel* means 'good news.' And the good news is this: When Jesus died on the cross for you and me, God reconciled us to himself and forgave us completely. Think about it. God is with us right now, and he isn't holding anything in his heart against us.

"Eric, are you sure that reconciliation and forgiveness came into God's heart the day Jesus died, because it doesn't *feel* that way to me." Unfortunately, that's true. It doesn't feel that way.

Imagine this. Two people are the best of friends. They do everything together. We would call them inseparable. But something happens and one betrays the other. They part ways. They live completely separate lives for many years. One day, news comes that the betrayer has died, and the other feels compelled to attend the funeral, where he breaks down emotionally. He falls against the casket and cries, "I'm here! I'm here!" Through his tears, he sobs, "I love you. I forgive you. I want us to be friends again." But the dead man can't respond.

God, in essence, is leaning over our casket. And he's very passionately speaking these same words to us. Reconciliation and forgiveness *did* come into the heart of God the day Jesus died on the cross, but because we're spiritually dead, we don't comprehend these spiritual realities.

"Did Jesus ever demonstrate that he had the ability to give us the salvation we need?"

Thankfully, God can do for us what the broken-hearted man only wishes he could do for his friend. God can bring us back to life by the same power that brought his only begotten Son back to life. Through the power of the Holy Spirit, who raised Jesus from the dead, we can be recreated in the image of God. That's what the phrase *born again* means. Rather than feeling separated from him, we can experience a reconciled relationship. Rather than thinking that we are condemned, we can know God's forgiveness and grace ... once we've dealt with the issue of our death.

Jesus died for our sins; his death equals our death. He demonstrated power over death by rising from the dead; his life can equal our life.

Is there another great moral teacher who was conceived by the Holy Spirit and born of a virgin; who died for the sins of the whole world; whose resurrection demonstrated his or her power to give life to spiritually dead people? If there is, maybe there's another way to get to God. But if not, it doesn't do us any good to stay offended at Jesus' claim to be the only way.

I think of my friend Craig's story. He was skeptical about Christianity, although his wife had been a Christian for several years and was a part of our ministry's early brainstorming sessions. Because Craig and I are personal friends, he accompanied his wife to many of these meetings, and for a few months he heard the message over and over. One day he called me during his drive home from work.

"Eric, this sounds completely crazy to me. But when you say that God talks to you, that you have a relationship with him, I believe you. I really do. But it brings up a nagging question. Why hasn't God ever spoken to me?" We visited for about a half an hour and talked about the very things we've looked at in the first chapters of this book.

I told him that people were created in the image of God to be like God, to experience a relationship with him forever. I explained that this doesn't happen naturally for any of us because of the effect of sin on all of us. Adam's sin caused the whole world to be separated from God. And the Law condemned all of us to die as sinners. At the eleventh hour, so to speak, Jesus Christ came and died in our place, and somehow his physical death resulted in our spiritual death. Also with his death came reconciliation and forgiveness, but this doesn't do dead people a lot of good. Jesus rose from the dead, and right this minute he's offering to give you life, spiritual life, as well.

Is this what you want? Are you willing to follow the only way to God? Do you want to begin your friendship with him? Are you willing to turn 180° from the sin in your life? Do you want to experience God's grace and forgiveness? The Holy Spirit will live inside you, changing your character and giving you the power to live with meaning and purpose. Is all of this what you want?

Craig told me that he needed time to process the information I had shared. And he did exactly that. I had the privilege of being with Craig just one week later as he prayed from his heart, committing his life to the Lord Jesus. Some people reading this book will sense a readiness right now to do the same. Is this the case for you?

If so, I'm going to ask you to do something which may seem strange and a bit uncomfortable. I'm about to ask you to stop reading and begin praying. Now you know about the salvation that is necessary to experience the relationship that is available. Now it's time to talk to God about it. The following questions may help prompt you as you pray your own personal prayer to God. After each paragraph, stop reading and pray.

- *Do you feel distant from God and guilty for your sin? Do you feel that the Holy Spirit is prompting to receive God's forgiveness and friendship? Respond to God in your own words.*

- *Are you thankful that Jesus paid your death penalty? Do you believe that God raised Jesus from the dead, and can give you life as well? Express your belief. Ask God to answer your questions and doubts.*

- *Do you want to become all that God wants you to be? Are you willing to give up control of your life, to follow the leading of the Holy Spirit? Offer a declaration of surrender. Welcome the Holy Spirit into your life.*

- *Are there any personal issues that you would like to talk to God about? Share from your heart. He wants to 'know you' because you want him to know you.*

If you feel that you would like to document your prayer and the experience of beginning your friendship with God, please do so below.

_____

_____

_____

_____

_____

_____

_____

_____

_____

_____

If you've prayed to accept salvation as a result of this material,
we'd love to hear from you. Please contact us at:
Faith@EricHolmesMinistries.org

* * *

NOTE: Further suggestions are offered on pages 52-53 for people who are not yet ready to receive salvation; and on pages 54-56 for those who have taken the last few moments to receive Jesus as Savior and Lord.

The Extra Effort (Search & Rescue)

Have you ever been offended by Jesus' claim to be the only way to God? Have you ever found something that Jesus said or did difficult to believe? If so, what is it and why?

Many people, including some Christians, do not believe that Jesus lived a sinless life on earth. If these people were correct, what effect would this belief have on Christianity?

How well do you accept God's love for you personally? If you find it difficult, what do you think could cause God to love you more?

Part II: Study the Maps

*   *   *

∞ If you can, note a recent news story, as well as a personal story, that relates to topics in this chapter.

News: ....

Personal: ....

∞ List two things that impacted you as you read the chapter or participated in a group discussion.

....

....

....

Scoring for *Search & Rescue* discussion groups:

    Read-4 ∗ Notes-8 ∗ News-1 ∗ Personal-2 ∗ Impact-16 ∗ Total-_____

Resolution in a Weekend?

Is it possible that we were created to be like God and meant to be with him forever? Is it likely that our sin has led, not only to separation from our Creator, but to our spiritual death as well?

If you feel that the answer to these questions *could* be yes, and you're willing to entertain the idea that the crucifixion and resurrection of Jesus Christ *may* be the only way out of the mess we're in, then it's important to resolve the issue of your belief and obedience to Jesus. Your 'barely a search' for truth must be fanned into an earnest search, a desperate search.

I mentioned in the chapter that my friend Craig needed time to process everything we talked about. You may need time, too. Maybe resolution for you will come within a week, like it did for Craig, or within several months, like it has for many others. In any case, it would be in your best interest to throw yourself into the process right now.

And know this; truth isn't found in only one single resource. Craig told me that "it wasn't a single instance but a collection of events. It may have been a conversation, a verse from the Bible, a lesson from my business course at college, a passage from [author] Lee Strobel, the visual impact of *The Passion of the Christ*, a message from a Sunday sermon, or some combination of all these things. I'm not sure what it was specifically, and at this point it's irrelevant to me. The point is that something did click the light on. Everything in my life suddenly is connected. There is purpose."

I want to challenge you to embark on what I'll call *A Resolution Quest*. Understand that this isn't a casual approach to finding truth. It will take the motivation of an earnest search to accomplish this. It can be done in a weekend, Friday night through Sunday, but you should walk through it at your own pace.

If you're willing to take me up on my challenge, you'll need a copy of *The Passion of the Christ* movie and Lee Strobel's book *The Case for Easter*. (The material in this small book is also Chapters 11-13 in the book *The Case for Christ*. You can use either book.) You'll also need a pen and a notepad for journaling.

I've outlined the details regarding *A Resolution Quest* on the next page.

My hope and prayer is that things will fall into place for you by the end of your quest. It may. One thing is certain though; you will have seen and heard the message of the gospel almost as fully as possible. And you will know exactly what it is you are embracing or rejecting.

A Resolution Quest

☐ WATCH *The Passion of the Christ.*
Afterwards, journal your thoughts for at least 15 minutes.

READ *The Case for Easter* (or the 3 chapters in *The Case for Christ*).
Journal for at least five to ten minutes after each of the following
reading sessions.

☐ THE MEDICAL EVIDENCE
Resurrection or Resuscitation?
The Tenth Interview
The Torture Before the Cross
The Agony of the Cross
The Cause of Death

☐ THE MEDICAL EVIDENCE
Answering the Skeptics
The Final Argument
A Question for the Heart
THE EVIDENCE OF THE MISSING BODY
The Eleventh Interview
Defending the Empty Tomb

☐ THE EVIDENCE OF THE MISSING BODY
Was Jesus Really Buried in the Tomb?
Is Joseph of Arimathea Historical?
How Secure Was the Tomb?
Were Any Guards Present?
What About the Contradictions?

☐ THE EVIDENCE OF THE MISSING BODY
Can Discrepancies be Harmonized?
Can the Witnesses be Trusted?
Why Did the Women Visit the Tomb?
Why Didn't Christians Cite the Empty Tomb?
What's the Affirmative Evidence?
What About Alternative Theories?
Conclusion: The Tomb Was Vacant

☐ THE EVIDENCE OF APPEARANCES
The Twelfth Interview
"Dead People Don't Do That"
"Convince Me It's a Creed"
The Mystery of the Five Hundred

☐ THE EVIDENCE OF APPEARANCES
The Testimony of the Gospels
Mark's Missing Conclusion
Are There Any Alternatives?
"No Rational Doubt"
The Resurrection of Debbie

People accept salvation through Jesus Christ for various reasons, but the ultimate reason should be to begin a relationship with God. You may remember the story of my "non-encounter" with a false prophet and my prayer of re-commitment to God afterwards. *God, from now on I'll do whatever you ask me to do.* That should be our prayer of commitment to God when we start, rather than when we blow it, like I did.

There are times when we can describe our life as a Christian as 'my questions and God's answers.' On other occasions, it will be 'God's initiative and my response.' Either way, God is the source of what's best for us, and it's our obedience to what he wants which actually leads to our best life. Christians are 'followers of God,' and built right into this new life of ours is a first act of obedience—being baptized in water.

Baptism doesn't add anything to our salvation, but it's very important and powerful. It symbolizes our death, burial, and resurrection with Christ. Now it's true that all people are born into this world living under the effects of death and burial, but we haven't experienced the resurrection of Jesus until we commit our lives to him and are born again. Therefore, baptism is a symbolic, public showing of a completed cycle: from created in the image of God, to being crucified with Christ, to being recreated in the image of God. In essence, baptism says, "Let everyone know and understand that I am now complete in Jesus Christ!"

I've baptized people in various places: from an outdoor hot tub in the month of January, to the baptismal tank of the First Baptist Church my grandparents attended. Together, my wife and I baptized our daughter in a junior high swimming pool. God isn't concerned about where someone is baptized as much as he is about our declaration to others and the experience of his presence.

I baptized a woman in her aunt and uncle's backyard Jacuzzi. She had been a Christian for awhile but had never experienced this wonderful symbol of her faith in Jesus. I remember the moment she came up out of the water. She felt the presence of God to such a strong degree that she began crying uncontrollably. She held tightly to her aunt and uncle, apologizing to them for mocking their Christianity in her younger years. Miracles, small and large, can take place when people are baptized.

People have been baptized in several traditional ways, but I love the symbolism of our "burial through baptism" mentioned in Romans 6:4, so I choose to immerse, or dunk people completely underwater.

Also, we know that many people have been baptized because of the tradition of infant baptism. This may surprise some, but I love the potential of this concept; understanding, though, that the infant isn't baptized because of *their* decision, but because of their parents' decision. The baptism doesn't take place because of the child's commitment, but because of the parents' commitment to raise the child in such a way that the teachings of Jesus are always near. So, when the day comes that the Holy Spirit draws this young person to Christ, he or she can make their own decision, their own commitment to respond and be born again. And having done this, they can begin their relationship with God, also believing and obeying his command to be baptized. Whether our parents were faithful to their commitment or not, we can be thankful that God was faithful to his part in our life.

You know, it sometimes seems as though we have a choice as to whether or not we'll be baptized, because not all Christians choose to follow this command. But the truth is, if we've made a commitment to obey God in everything, why would we choose to not obey his command to be baptized? It simply doesn't make sense.

If you're doing this Bible study with a group, you can ask if the leader or maybe even the leader's pastor would be willing to baptize you. For those of you reading this book on your own, maybe it will work out best to be baptized once you begin attending a church.

And speaking of church, there are some basics to know which will help you as you begin your friendship with God. I *could* suggest that your growth as a follower of Jesus depends on your ability to read the Bible, pray, go to church, serve others, and share your faith. I could, but it isn't true. Your growth as a Christian depends on your interaction with the Holy Spirit, your connection to him ... as you read the Bible, as you pray, as you go to church, as you serve, as you share your faith, and so much more.

There's a lot to say about these issues. And this is exactly what we're going to do in upcoming chapters of the *8 Great Wonders*, so stay tuned.

As I close, I want to say a few words about the fact that you've felt the tug of God on your heart and have responded by praying your own prayer to be born again.

The Bible teaches that if we confess Jesus as Lord and believe in our heart that God raised him from the dead, we will be saved[16]. This is a rock-solid promise from God. You will never again have to decide whether or not you want to receive life from him, but every day you will have to choose to live the life that you've been given. In the next chapter we'll talk more about salvation and what happens next.

Until then, I would suggest starting to get to know your Savior better. You can do this by reading one of the biographies of Jesus in the Bible: Matthew, Mark, Luke, or John. Personally, I recommend the Gospel of John, and after that the Book of Romans. Each time, as you begin to read, ask the Holy Spirit to teach you. Ask him to speak to you. You'll begin to see your friendship take shape in no time.

I want to end with a prayer for you.

Dear God, thank you for the message of a reconciled relationship with you. Thank you for salvation through Jesus in the face of emptiness and eternal death.

Lord, I ask on behalf of this person who has prayed to receive life through Jesus, that you would fill them with the power of your Holy Spirit. I pray that he would speak to them clearly and that he would protect them from the negative words that are bound to be spoken by those who don't yet know you. Let this person's new life and words draw those around them into a friendship with you as well.

Give this new friend of yours a strong desire to read the Bible, to know more about Jesus, and to learn more about the new person they themselves are destined to become.

Thank you so much, Jesus. In your name I pray. Amen.

God really has blessed you in your discoveries, hasn't he?
Congratulations.

[1] John 14:2-6

[2] Matthew 5:39, Luke 6:29

[3] Matthew 7:1, Luke 6:37

[4] Matthew 6:9-13

[5] Matthew 14:15-21, Mark 6:34-44, Luke 9:12-17, John 6:5-14

[6] Luke 10:30-37

[7] Luke 15:11-32

[8] Hebrews 4:15b

[9] Matthew 1:18-25

[10] M. R. DeHaan, <u>The Chemistry of the Blood and Other Stirring Messages</u> (Grand Rapids: Zondervan, 1943), 31.

[11] Romans 5:9

[12] Ephesians 1:7

[13] Revelation 5:9

[14] 1 John 1:7

[15] Hebrews 9:6-26

[16] Romans 10:9

5 ❧ Spirit, Soul, and Body

Salvation is experienced.

Wayne, the Guy from the Carport

Early in our marriage, when my wife and I were still living in our apartment, there was a young couple who parked next to us under the carport. From time to time we would see each other there and say hi, but that's about as far as it went.

I was working temporary jobs at the time and one of my assignments was for a company that had a major and immediate project coming up. But the project didn't materialize during the few days I was there. As I waited for glitches to be ironed out, the only thing I accomplished was ... meeting and visiting briefly with Wayne, the guy from the carport. I thought it was quite a coincidence that he worked there.

Once I moved on to my next job assignment, our relationship went back to the crossing of paths as one of us was leaving home and the other was returning; although now I could say, "Hi, *Wayne*."

Several months went by, and one day, as we were pulling in, Wayne was pacing on the sidewalk. He had a nervous look in his eye as he walked up to me and said, "The Holy Spirit told me to talk to you."

Wayne began sharing with me that he was a Christian whose life was spiraling out of control.

He and I spent a lot of time together over the next few weeks. I listened as a confused and sometimes angry man tried to make sense out of things that were happening in his life. I did my best to support and encourage him when I could.

Wayne joined us as we hosted a Christian book study with another couple. We were reading and discussing *Classic Christianity*[1], a book which had impacted my life.

Through our discussions I realized that, although Wayne had experienced salvation through Jesus, he didn't understand salvation. And his lack of understanding actually contributed to the negative turn his life had taken.

Over time, as he began to understand the truth of what it means to be a saved person, the fog began to lift from Wayne's mind. He took the message to heart and began sharing it with others. His confidence grew. He began to hear God's voice clearly again. Ultimately, through a series of incredible and, quite frankly, miraculous personal events, God restored the life that had been slipping away from Wayne. It was a wonderful outcome to his story.

> Although people experience salvation, many don't understand it. And this lack of understanding can have a negative effect in our lives.

As I think about the story though, I can't seem to shake this statement: "Although he had experienced salvation, he didn't understand it; and it had a negative effect in his life." I've seen this story of Wayne's play out in the lives of others as well.

I guess there are any number of reasons why people have chosen to become Christians. I've heard good answers; like "to go to heaven," and "to change my life around and get my wife back." But rarely do I hear the reason that God had in mind when he decided to offer us salvation in the first place; that is, to begin and develop a personal relationship with him. Although many of us Christians have heard the phrase *relationship with God*, few of us have ever been told what it means. We've barely even seen what it looks like.

Hopefully, you've seen enough in this book to begin to realize that a relationship with God is a series of 'God experiences.' He answers prayer, he teaches, he sets people free, he speaks and calls people to serve, he saves and protects, he leads people back to himself, and that's just for starters.

The time has come for us to add knowledge to our experience of salvation, so that we can also add the on-going experiences of a relationship with God. In doing this, we will see the connection between the sixth, seventh and eighth great wonders: <u>*your name* Accepts Salvation</u>, <u>*your name* Lives by Faith</u>, and *God and People, Together Forever*.

I've witnessed the moment that the teaching in this chapter clicks in the heart and mind of person after person. I've seen it in their eyes.

One Sunday morning I had my big chance to share this lesson with a crowd of about 75 or so. I had three members of the church's drama team behind me, wearing t-shirts I had made. Kathy wore a white t-shirt with the word *SPIRIT* on the front. Aaron stood next to her wearing a gray shirt with the word *SOUL*. And next to him was Ken in a black shirt with the word *BODY*. As I gave the talk that morning, these three actors demonstrated the connection, the salvation, and the struggle of our spirit, soul, and body.

I love success stories. Unfortunately, this isn't exactly one of them. I completely blew my opportunity that morning. Convinced I absolutely knew my material inside and out, I chose not to prepare an outline. I was "shot-gunning it," as one of the actors told me later. I was so all-over-the-place I actually heard the Holy Spirit say, *You're done*, as if I was being pulled off the stage with a long hook. And yet, several people told me afterwards that the teaching had answered questions for them that no one had ever addressed before. So I know that this teaching can be impacting for anyone, and maybe more so if I bury my ego and follow an outline.

The first thing I want to do is to identify the spirit, soul, and body—which sounds easy enough. Then we're going to look at how salvation affects the three parts of every person at different times and in different ways. Finally, we're going to see why this concept is so powerfully relevant to people like my neighbor Wayne, and to you and me as well.

In the Bible, two distinct concepts define what a human being is: *outer appearance* and *inner self*. The word *body*, of course, is used most often to refer to our outer appearance. And two words, *soul* and *spirit*, are commonly used to define our inner self.

I've heard soul and spirit described as conjoined twins. Just as it would take many hours of intricate surgery to separate conjoined siblings, the Bible says that the separation of the soul and spirit would also be intricate and can only be accomplished by God's Word itself[2].

Together, my dad and I once studied these two words, in the original language of the New Testament, to see if there's any distinction between them. This is almost the entire extent of my knowledge of the Bible's original languages, so don't get nervous. Here's the essence of what I see on our five pages of notes, torn from a spiral notebook.

- The Greek word *psuchē* (soo-kay) means breath, the soul. It appears 36 times in the New Testament as the word *life* and 33 times as the word *soul*. Our notes are fairly cut and dry, and dad summarized it pretty well when he wrote at the bottom of one page; *person—personality—life—self—soul—the real you!*

- *Pneuma* (new-muh) means wind, spirit. It appears 239 times referring to the Holy Spirit (God) and 103 times referring to human spirit. The notes we jotted down are much more dynamic. For a Christian (an important distinction), the human spirit is the offspring of the Holy Spirit[3]. It's described as the spirit of an adopted child[4]. The human spirit worships God[5], and is provoked by idol worship[6]. It rejoices greatly[7]. Not only does it pray[8]; it's ready, willing, and eager to watch and pray[9]. The human spirit serves God[10], and a fervent spirit causes us to speak and teach about Jesus[11].

Dad and I drew the conclusion that the word spirit strongly implies a *religious self* and soul speaks more of a *personal self*, although the differences were not always black and white—bringing the idea of 'conjoined' back to mind.

At one of the national bookstore chains I noticed a selection of books and DVDs labeled *Mind, Spirit and Body*. And it dawned on me; each part of our humanity has a lot to do with healthy relationships. So based on what we discovered about these words from the Bible, here are some definitions I want to establish, not only for the chapter, but for the entire *8 Great Wonders* teaching.

- **Spirit**: our religious self. We were created *spiritually* to experience friendship with God.

From time to time I listen to a radio program that's hosted by two atheists who talk politics more than religion. I once heard these two men laughing about their inability to find the spirit inside them—"whatever that is," one of them said. Ironic, isn't it? The human spirit is meant to experience a relationship with God.

- **Soul**: our personal self. We were created *personally* to enjoy healthy relationships with other people. I like to describe the soul as *emotion*, *personality*, and *intellect*, but many other words also apply; like *heart*, *mind*, *thought*, *conscience*, *comprehension*—the list goes on and on.

How we treat others is incredibly important. People, in my opinion, are the most valuable thing on earth. And the best things about people are the experiences we can share and the stories we can tell.

- **Body**: our physical self with its five senses—sight, hearing, touch, taste, and smell. We were created *physically* to responsibly care for God's creation.

The human body is built to experience the goodness of the world around it in a healthy manner. In general, how we treat the earth, the water, and the air is as important as how we care for our own backyard gardens and family pets. And caring for our own bodies through nutrition and an active lifestyle can enhance every relationship we can experience.

Each of us is made up of spirit, soul, and body. These words appear in the Bible hundreds of times, but interestingly, there's only one verse in which we see all three together.

> ²³*Now may the God of peace Himself sanctify you entirely; and may your spirit and soul and body be preserved complete, without blame at the coming of our Lord Jesus Christ.*
>
> *1 Thessalonians 5:23*

"Complete, without blame." Think about that for a moment.

The very first time I taught the *8 Great Wonders* from our workbook, it was as a part of my daughter's school lessons. I remember her question, "Are there any people alive right now who are related to Adam and Eve?" She was amazed to learn that we're *all* related to Adam and Eve.

What a wonderful thing; a perfect friendship with God, perfect relationships with one another, and responsible care for the world around them. This is where we come from. This is our heritage as human beings.

If you took the opportunity to read *The What-Could-Have-Been Bible* mentioned in Chapter 2, you probably noticed that where we came from is also where we're meant to go. Question is: How do we get there from here?

Completely, More Each Day, and Not Yet

Let's begin a conversation about how we experience salvation. And let's start with a picture of the health and wholeness that comes from a personal relationship with God. It's a picture of six connected links: God the Father, Jesus Christ, and the Holy Spirit ... *connected to* ... a person's spirit, soul, and body.

$$\frac{\text{God}}{\text{Father, Son, } \textit{Holy Spirit}} \quad + \quad \frac{\text{Person}}{\textit{spirit}\text{, soul, body}}$$

We have to start here, with the three parts of every person, to understand salvation and the relationship we're meant to experience.

There's no such thing as a completely whole person outside of a relationship with God. And there's no such thing as a relationship with God unless our spirit is born again, which reconnects us to God through the Holy Spirit.

I heard about a country preacher who had an interesting response to the question, "Are you saved?" His answer was, "Completely, more and more each day, and not yet." He understood that biblical salvation affects the spirit, soul, and body of a person in different ways and at different times.

Being born again, connected to the Holy Spirit, points to our initial need for salvation. Remember Romans 6:6? *Our old self was crucified with Christ.* It wasn't our physical self that was crucified. None of us were born with scars in our wrists and feet. It wasn't our personal self that died with Christ. We're all born with a living soul (emotion, personality, and intellect). So we have to ask ourselves: Could the "old self" be referring to our spirit? How many of us are born into this world already knowing God personally? The answer is none of us. That's why Jesus said that we must be born again[12], because that which is born of the Holy Spirit is spirit[13].

We're born into this world with a living body and a living soul, but a dead spirit. And although God is right here with us, there's no connection to him because of this deadness. Everything about biblical salvation points first to our spirit's need to be born of God.

Our spirit experiences a *moment* of salvation. Being born of God is instantaneous and complete. The scholarly word is *regeneration*. And when it happens, the Holy Spirit also comes to live inside the new Christian. John, one of Jesus' Apostles, tells us in one of his writings that no one who is born of God practices sin, because God's seed remains in him, and he cannot sin because he is born of God[14]. *God's seed*, mentioned here, is our spirit. Paul taught that, with the new birth, comes a new identity. We actually "become the righteousness of God in Christ[15]." This is also a reference to our spirit.

So, our spirit experiences salvation first.

Next, beginning at the moment of spiritual salvation and continuing through the remainder of our life, our soul can experience a *process* of salvation. Paul refers to this as 'becoming like Jesus, as our thinking and behavior are changed[16].' The scholarly word is *sanctification*. This happens as we approach spiritual disciplines—Bible reading, prayer, attending church, etc.—with an expectancy to hear, believe, and obey the Holy Spirit. Over time, as we experience a friendship with God in this way, he develops our character and reveals our calling in life. Although the process is simple, it's not always easy. When it feels as if I'm taking 'two steps forward and one step—*or more*—back,' that's when I find some of the *Principles of a Wonderful Trip* very helpful. It's good to look at those from time to time.

So, our spirit can be born again, and our soul can be developed to become more and more like Jesus. But there's even more good news. Our body can also be saved.

No one has experienced the salvation of the body ... yet. But God has promised that the Holy Spirit living inside us is a guarantee of our physical salvation[17]. Our body will experience this finalizing salvation, so to speak, the moment Jesus returns for us[18]. Our body will be made perfect, immortal and incorruptible[19], just like it was when Adam walked in the Garden of Eden and when Jesus walked from the empty tomb. The scholarly word is *glorification*.

> Our *spirit* experiences a moment of salvation. Then, our *soul* experiences a process of salvation. And one day, our *body* will experience an instant, finalizing salvation.

Although I've just described three parts to salvation, touching the three parts of every person, there's a Greek word that pulls all of this together in one wonderful package. The word is *sōzō* (sounds like it's written), which means *made whole*. If you and I choose to believe God's message and begin a personal friendship with him, then it's God's agenda for us to be completely restored— spirit, soul, and body. What an incredible thought.

The Battle for 'Undecided'

As we head down the home stretch, I want to make sure that we understand something. What we've talked about so far is all well and good, but it isn't relevant yet. It won't impact us until we know how to bring these truths into our lives so that they can make a difference when we wake up tomorrow morning. Please follow me for a few more minutes.

The three most important participants in a debate are the two debaters and the person who hasn't made up his or her mind yet—also known, during election years, as 'Undecided.' During a debate, the two presenters aren't trying to convince one another of their positions. And they aren't really trying to pull audience members who hold the opposite view over to their way of thinking. The goal of a good debater is to appeal to Mr. or Ms. Undecided.

I understood this the night I saw the debate I mentioned in Chapter 1. When the atheist said that he wouldn't consider himself to be an atheist, he was just someone who *doubted* the existence of the Christian God, I prayed a silent prayer of protection for all the Christians in the audience who could identify with that statement, who struggle with doubt.

Sometimes living as a Christian can seem like a struggle because of the debate; not the publicized one at the venue down the street, but the debate inside of us every day of our lives.

Ken and I met over breakfast one morning. (Yes, the same Ken who would later act out these principles with Kathy and Aaron.) That morning, he confessed some of his darkest struggles with sin. He told me that he had accepted Christ as his Savior when he was a child. And he said that, growing up in church, he knew all the teachings and practices of Christianity. But, like Wayne in the story which opened this chapter, Ken was a Christian whose life was out of control. In his own words[20]:

> I'm a person who has had a roller coaster ride in my relationship with God since I can remember. I'm a person who wishes he could just find out what it is he's supposed to do with his life and be happy about it. I'm a person who's afraid to be alone with his thoughts. I'm a person who's so consumed with his sin that it inhibits me from being who God has called me to be.
>
> Am I doomed to the life I'm now in? Is there a way out? Where would I be if I followed what God had laid out for me for the past 10 to 15 years? One thing is absolutely certain—I cannot continue down the road I am currently on. My depression and sin will only increase, and I will end up an old man

wondering where my life went. I don't ever want to play the 'what if' game. Unfortunately, I already am.

Quite honestly, it was an emotional moment for both of us as Ken described his depression and the sin which led to it. I respectfully asked for and was given permission to respond. So I set three orange juice glasses in front of us. "This first one is our spirit. This next one is our soul. And this last one is our body."

Here's what I shared.

At the near end of the three glasses is our born-again spirit. It cannot sin. It embraces everything that God communicates.

At the far end is our body, or "the flesh" as the Bible refers to it. It's selfish and can't do right. The flesh is driven by what it sees, hears, touches, tastes, and smells. And as much as our spirit is the righteousness of God, our flesh is the wretchedness of man.

Stuck in the middle, being pulled by both the spirit and the flesh, is our soul, which has some decisions to make.

5For those who are according to the flesh set their minds on the things of the flesh, but those who are according to the Spirit, the things of the Spirit. 6For the mind set on the flesh is death, but the mind set on the Spirit is life and peace, 7because the mind set on the flesh is hostile toward God; for it does not subject itself to the law of God, for it is not even able to do so, 8and those who are in the flesh cannot please God.

9However, you are not in the flesh but in the Spirit, if indeed the Spirit of God dwells in you. But if anyone does not have the Spirit of Christ, he does not belong to Him. 10If Christ is in you, though the body is dead because of sin, yet the spirit is alive because of righteousness. 11But if the Spirit of Him who raised Jesus from the dead dwells in you, He who raised Christ Jesus from the dead will also give life to your mortal bodies through His Spirit who dwells in you.

12So then, brethren, we are under obligation, not to the flesh, to live according to the flesh—13for if you are living according to the flesh, you must die; but if by the Spirit you are putting to death the deeds of the body, you will live. 14For all who are being led by the Spirit of God, these are sons of God. 15For you have not received a spirit of slavery leading to fear again, but you have received a spirit of adoption as sons by which we cry out, "Abba! Father!" 16The Spirit Himself testifies with our spirit that we are children of God, 17and if children, heirs also, heirs of God and fellow heirs with Christ, if indeed we suffer with Him so that we may also be glorified with Him.   *Romans 8:5-17*

I made sure that Ken understood that *fleshly-minded* is when our soul bases decisions on the urges of the body and its five senses. Whether it's deviant behavior, addictive vices, or simple selfishness, the mission statement of the flesh is: *If it feels good, do it.*

Being *spiritually-minded* is when the soul makes decisions based on communication between the Holy Spirit and our spirit. *If it's God's will, do it.*

The battle between the spirit and the flesh is on-going and rough because, no matter how spiritual we would like to become, our flesh will never lie down and die. But, thank God, neither will the Holy Spirit give up on speaking God's will into our lives.

Have you ever heard anything like this? "And that guy calls himself a Christian! Christians don't do things like that."

Before we became a Christian, being fleshly-minded was all we knew. Every one of our decisions was based on what we saw, heard, touched, tasted, and smelled. For those who come to Christ at an early age, there may not be years and years of life experience that was fleshly, but for others there may be decades of *stinkin' thinkin'* that have to be overcome. Thankfully, according to Romans 8, which we just read, it can be.

> Becoming a Christian does not erase years of selfish living, but living in the Holy Spirit can.

What I'm about to describe may sound far-fetched, but it's based on principles from Scripture. It's a scene from our own lives.

Satan, "the serpent of old[21]," tempts us to commit sin. Despite the fact that we know better, we look around to make sure no one see us, and we do it. Immediately, Satan accuses us[22]. He points us out to God and says, "Look! Your *child* is betraying you. You couldn't possibly love a sinner like that." He whispers something similar in our ears as well.

But Jesus Christ is also standing there. The Bible calls him our intercessor[23]; our defense lawyer, so to speak. He shows God the Father the nail prints in his wrists, and says, "The death penalty for sin has already been paid."

God brings down the gavel against Satan's accusation and declares, "Not guilty![24]" (We love a story like this, don't we?)

As Satan slams his briefcase and curses his way out of the courtroom, the Father calls Jesus over for a private talk. "Tell my child to stop it![25]"

Read that last statement again.

Jesus communicates God's will to us through the Holy Spirit, and the next thing you know we're feeling very uneasy about our sin. Not condemned, but convicted. God wants us to repent. He very strongly wants us to stop following our fleshly desires and to start obeying the Holy Spirit.

Doesn't this sound wonderful and easy? *Just stop it. Just say no.* You and I know it's not that easy. We know that the flesh isn't going to go away.

It's not enough that we know how all this works. "Knowing this" isn't going to change our lives; not until we change our minds and yield to God. Truthfully, *how much* and *how fast* we grow as a Christian is directly tied to how often we say yes to the Holy Spirit and no to our selfish, sinful desires.

If we become a 'living yes' to the Holy Spirit[26], we will see him develop our character and reveal our calling in life. And that's the key to everything.

Let's make up our minds that we're going to open the Bible, and pray, and hang out with God's people, and serve, and share our faith with others—all with the purpose of experiencing the God who calls us into this personal relationship with himself. Let's be intentional about experiencing God.

As we wake up in the morning we can pray a powerful prayer: *Lord, fill me with the power of your Holy Spirit today.* We can pray it because we want the strength in our lives to come in the area of our spiritual-mindedness, not our fleshliness. And we can pray it because God wants us to grow up and become like Christ.

> A life of meaning and purpose begins when we become a *living yes* to the Holy Spirit.

[29]For those whom [God] *foreknew, He also predestined to become conformed to the image of His Son, so that He would be the firstborn among many brethren; ...*

Romans 8:29

Sometimes I can actually feel a strong sense behind this message, and I have to remember that it can be a bit overwhelming for people. I asked Ken if he was okay, but I could see it in his eyes.

"After 20 years of being saved," he said, "I have hope for the first time that Christ can save me from my sinful body, and that it will happen through my relationship with God."

Before he left, Ken told me, "If people could see what I've just seen, their lives would be absolutely transformed."

Based on my own life and the lives of others, I would have to agree.

The Extra Effort (Search & Rescue)

  🙢 Describe how you are currently growing in your a) *spiritual* relationship with God, b) *personal* relationships with others, and in c) your responsible care of the *physical* world (yourself and your environment).

_____

_____

_____

     The information in the diagram below shows the state of our spirit, our soul, and our body as the human race progressed through the *8 Great Wonders* as they originally happened. For example, as a result of the event *God Creates People*, people were loving God spiritually, loving others personally, and fully alive physically. Then, after the event *People Sin Against God*, we were separated from him spiritually, growing selfish personally, and in the process of dying physically—quite a fall.

salvation	*Spiritually* (Spirit—the image of God; for friendship with God)	*Personally* (Soul—emotion, personality, intellect; for healthy relationships with people)	*Physically* (Body—the five senses; experiencing God's world)
As a result of:	People are:	People are:	People are:
God Creates People	Loving God	Loving others	Fully Alive
People Sin Against God	Separated	Separated, selfish	Separated, dying
God's Law Is Given	Condemned	Condemned, selfish	Condemned, dying
Jesus Christ Dies	Dead	Reconciled/forgiven, selfish	Dying
Jesus, Alive Again!	Dead, offered Life	Reconciled/forgiven, selfish	Dying
... Accepts Salvation	Reborn, w/Holy Spirit	Able to love	Immortality promised
... Lives by Faith	Living in the Holy Spirit	Growing in love	Immortality promised
... Together Forever	Loving God	Matured by love	Changed, like Jesus

Revelation 20:11-15

... Rejects Salvation	Dead, offered Life	Reconciled/forgiven, selfish	Dying
... Lives for Self	Dead, offered Life	Reconciled/forgiven, selfish	Dying
... Separated Forever	Dead	In the Lake of Fire	Dead

❧ If the *8 Great Wonders* have had, or can have, the same effect on every human being (as the diagram shows), then how can there be two incredibly opposite outcomes? How would you explain the difference?

....

....

....

❧ Wayne and Ken both experienced salvation, and then understood what it means. So, based on Romans 8, what comes next for them and for us as well?

....

....

....

* * *

❧ If you can, note a recent news story, as well as a personal story, that relates to topics in this chapter.

News: ....

Personal: ....

❧ List two things that impacted you as you read the chapter or participated in a group discussion.

....

....

....

Scoring for *Search & Rescue* discussion groups:

*Read-4 * Notes-8 * News-1 * Personal-2 * Impact-16 * Total-_____*

[1] Bob George, <u>Classic Christianity: Life's Too Short to Miss the Real Thing</u> (Eugene: Harvest House, 1989).

[2] Hebrews 4:12

[3] John 3:6

[4] Romans 8:15

[5] John 4:23

[6] Acts 17:16

[7] Luke 1:47

[8] Ephesians 6:18

[9] Matthew 26:41

[10] Romans 1:9

[11] Acts 18:25

[12] John 3:3

[13] John 3:6

[14] 1 John 3:9

[15] 2 Corinthians 5:21

[16] Romans 8:29, Romans 12:2

[17] Ephesians 1:13-14

[18] 1 John 3:2

[19] 1 Corinthians 15:51-53

[20] *"I'm a person who ... Unfortunately, I already am."*: Edited from an actual entry in Ken's journal. Printed with permission.

[21] Revelation 12:9

[22] Revelation 12:10

[23] Romans 8:34, Hebrews 7:25

[24] Romans 8:33

[25] John 16:8-13

[26] see Romans 12:1

Spirit, Soul, and Body

6 ❧ Before We Break Camp

Someone's Personal Journal Opens

So far, we've moved from *interesting* to *challenging*. We began at 30,000 feet, with an overview of what it's all about—a relationship with God. At the base camp we studied the maps—the connections between certain great wonders—and we were invited to commit ourselves to the adventure of a lifetime.

Are we ready to move forward?

What we're about to read can be viewed as someone's personal journal. If we choose to let these words be an experienced arm around our shoulder as we begin our journey, I believe we'll be positioned and prepared to move from *challenging* to *impacting*.

* * *

2-18-01:

During his leadership presentation this afternoon, Dr. John Maxwell spoke some of the most profound words I've ever heard. He told us that there are three circumstances under which people will change for the better: when someone hurts enough to have to change, when they learn enough to want to change, and when they receive enough support from someone else to be able to change.

Looking back, I realize that there has been a catalyst behind every major change in my life. I'm convinced that the three circumstances Dr. Maxwell identified today define my journey so far.

I've been supported enough to be able to change.

Summer, 1983:

I still can't believe what happened.

This afternoon, a Bible teacher asked me to share my belief regarding Judgment Day.

So I told him that I believed that one day each of us will stand before God and be held accountable for how we lived our lives. One of the Bible passages I referred to was Matthew 25:31-34 & 41.

He asked me what I thought the standard will be that God will use when he judges us.

"It'll be the Bible. Did I love God with everything in me ... and my neighbor too? Did I 'not steal,' 'not murder,' 'not commit adultery'?"

We discussed whether or not God will judge us for beliefs not found in the Bible; like believing whether the Shroud of Turin is the burial cloth of Jesus or not. I thought that question was a good one.

He said, "The resurrection of Jesus is clearly spelled out in Scripture, but the identification of his burial cloth isn't. So, is there anything that God expects every person, from everywhere in the world, from every period in history to know and believe that's not spelled out in the Bible?"

Up to this point I thought we were talking about Judgment Day. Then he asked, "What are your thoughts on how the world began?"

I was a little excited to be able to share my views, having spent a lot of time studying the topic.

"I believe that God spoke and there was a big bang." I talked about the millions of years from the formation of single-celled life, to dinosaurs, to cave men. I mentioned that it seemed to me that God must not have been too pleased with the way things were going because he caused an ice age, that even the Bible says that the earth was "formless and void." What came next must have been 'God's Do-Over,' when He created Adam and Eve.

"Eric, how much of what you just said is found in the Bible—the standard God will use to judge your beliefs?"

Ouch! "Not too much."

Then he dropped the bomb. "God requires you to believe just a few words of your belief system. If he doesn't require you to believe the rest of it, isn't it okay to let it go?"

I was dumbfounded. He didn't say that my belief was *wrong*. He just said that most of my belief wasn't *necessary*. I stood there motionless as the logic sank in. And I couldn't think of one single reason to disagree. His words still echo in my mind.

"Isn't it okay to let it go?"

I've hurt enough to have to change.

5-14-91, day 1:

We were expecting my sister around 7:00 pm. I decided to wait for her by the Emergency Room parking lot.

I began thinking about what God could be doing in this situation. I wasn't questioning God; I was just saying, *based on my knowledge of who he is and how he works—his mercy, his love, his righteousness, his grace ...*

I thought about how Jesus, in order to conquer death, had submitted himself to it. Maybe what the Lord is doing here is subjecting Dad to disease in order to conquer it once and for all in his life. If that's true, disease has taken Dad as far as it can. I know that God will restore his life and bring him back to us.

Then again, I don't really feel like I know anything right now.

Before I went back upstairs to the waiting room, I prayed.

5-28-91, day 15:

I'm having a bit of a problem ... with the thought that God would save Dad's life only to have him on medication for a long time ... and even though I don't understand it—maybe that's the way God wants it, he doesn't want me to understand ... but ... I almost feel like I've sort of been in control lately and ... I'm not the one who's supposed to be in control ... so I think God wants me to simply make notes of what's going on. Don't try to understand it. Don't try to make it go the way I think it should go. I'm going to step ... I'm going to say this in faith ... Jesus Christ is Lord. He knows what he's doing, and he is building a testimony.

6-20-91, day 38:

Before I got out of bed this morning, I was thinking about all the times the psalmist asked, "How long, O Lord?" [Psalm 6:3, 13:1-2, 35:17, 74:10, 89:46, 90:13, 94:3.]

God doesn't have a history of doing everything at the snap of a finger. He does things in his timing. We don't have the right to say, "Okay, it's time to heal me." Jesus healed a woman who had hemorrhaged for 12 years. He healed a woman whom Satan had bound for 18 years. He healed a man at the pool of Bethesda who had been sick for 38 years.

6-23-91—Day 41:

Last night I said to Francine, "Now that it's very late and we need to get some sleep, how would you like to talk?"

Basically, I spilled my guts about being afraid that if Dad doesn't get healed, then our belief system is right out the window. And if that's true, then nothing about my understanding of God's Word makes sense.

She said that the Holy Spirit just wants us to let go of things and let God do what he's doing. Don't try to second-guess it. Don't try to figure him out, which is what I've been doing most of the time.

Thank you, God, for bringing Francine into my life. She makes a lot of sense.

Sometime in July, 1991:

I was pacing and preaching in the apartment this morning. It was awesome. The end tables had already accepted Christ and the sofa was just about ready to surrender as well. I say that jokingly, but it really was an amazing time.

I don't remember exactly what I was preaching, but suddenly, words came out of my mouth that I had never heard before. "We try to make the written Word of God do what only the living Word of God can do." It stopped me dead in my tracks. I repeated it slowly. "I try to make ... the written Word of God ... do what only ... the living Word of God—the Holy Spirit ... can do." I fell to my knees and began crying.

I realize now that I've been depending on the black ink on the white pages of the Bible to save me, heal me, and free me. And I've forgotten that I have a living Savior, a personal Savior to make me whole.

I've also learned enough to be able to change.

Sometime in 1998:

Jesus coined the phrase *from the foundation of the world*. It appears in the Bible only seven times. In addition to Jesus, four of his Apostles used it in their writings.

- Matthew, in Matthew 13:34-35 (in which he quotes Psalm 78:2)
- Peter, in 1 Peter 1:20
- John, in Revelation 13:8 and 17:8
- Paul, in Ephesians 1:3-4

These four men are responsible for writing at least 21 of the 27 books of the New Testament. And what they wrote suggests that plans were already in God's heart regarding the human race before he even created us.

- As a sacrifice for our sins, Jesus Christ is the Lamb who has been slain *from the foundation of the world*.
- Christians' names are written in the Book of Life *from the foundation of the world*.
- God chose us in Christ *before the foundation of the world*, that we would be holy and blameless before him.
- There is a kingdom prepared for Christians *from the foundation of the world*.

* * *

Change happens in the life of a maturing Christian. Underline that word *maturing*. It's an important one.

The Holy Spirit can bring change into our lives through circumstances or other people. He can work from the outside in. But mostly, I think he would rather work from the inside out. He would rather change our thinking and our hearts as we intentionally search for him, as we question him. Change is the bridge between challenge and impact; uncomfortable, maybe, but certainly true.

I've shared three moments of great change in my life as I learned to take God at his word. What I see in them now is a sense of purpose. Take another look at those last four bullet points. I never could have learned that lesson while holding on to a belief system, only a few words of which are found in the Bible. And if I had rejected the idea of believing God rather than my own foolish interpretations, the *8 Great Wonders* teaching which has impacted my life so deeply, and the lives of others as well, may never have seen the light of day.

There's a simple-sounding, but tough question that I think we need to ask ourselves. Can we believe God 'just because he said so'?

When I was mixing biblical theology and secular theory, the answer for me was *no*. I somehow thought that 'knowing the truth' came from properly interpreting the Bible. And I did the best I could.

When I was focused only on the black ink on the white pages of the Bible, the answer was *sometimes*. Sometimes I could believe God because the Bible said so. But other times, I'd think, *If it's not in the Bible, to heck with it.* I would yield myself to the Holy Spirit's control in prayer, and then resist what that actually meant.

But after God began answering my "show me how everything fits together" prayer, my answer became a solid *yes* for the first time in my life. Yes, Lord, you can speak to me from every verse in the Bible, from every circumstance in my life, and from every person whose path I cross; even the verses, circumstances, and people I don't understand. Yes, Lord, you can speak to me.

Date unknown:

Francine and I came home from work late tonight. It was good to be home. She went into the kitchen, and I switched on the TV and sat down to relax. Not even five minutes later, this thought crossed my mind: *Hug your wife.* I thought it was a strange thing for God to say to me, but I got up and went into the kitchen. Francine melted into my arms when I hugged her.

"You have no idea how much I needed that."

Moments as simple as this are hanging in the balance as we begin our trek through the *8 Great Wonders*. Are we missing moments like these?

Check the Connections

Not too long ago my mom reminded me of one of those everyday truths of life: "When there's 'a disconnect' in the system, go back to the beginning and check each of the components until the problem is revealed." No big deal, right?

As soon as she said it, something clicked inside me, as though God had taken a highlighter to it. *Keep this in mind; it's important.*

Before the end of the day, Mom's reminder led me to an important discovery about the lessons behind each of the *8 Great Wonders*. These biblical teachings can and should be used as gauges, especially in regard to the following question: How's my friendship with God developing?

Here's an overview of what I'm talking about.

- ***God Creates People***

    Do I believe that people are built to experience a relationship with God? Can I take God at his word? Do I know my place before him? Am I the kind of worshipper he is seeking?

- ***People Sin Against God***

    Do I accept the fact that when I feel shame and distance between myself and God that it is a result of my sin? Have I come clean about the sin in my life and do I resist Satan's lies?

- ***God's Law Is Given***

    Do I try to close the distance I feel from God by living up to a list of do's and don'ts, or not? Do I know how the crucifixion of Jesus was God's antidote for the effects of the Law?

- ***Jesus Christ Dies***

    Do I understand that when Jesus died, everyone died with him? Do I believe that reconciliation and forgiveness came into God's heart completely the day Jesus died?

- ***Jesus, Alive Again!***

    Do I know the incredible hope that exists for us because Jesus was raised from the dead, as well as the dire hopelessness if he wasn't? Do I understand how Jesus is the only way to God?

- ***your name Accepts Salvation***

    Have I been born again? Do I understand the imperative for us to share our personal stories of faith until others become interested? Can I share the gospel message once someone is interested?

- ***your name Lives by Faith***

    Do I hear, believe, and obey the Holy Spirit? Do I create *faith opportunities* by reading the Bible, praying, and going to church? Is the Holy Spirit addressing my character? Is he revealing my calling?

- ***God and People, Together Forever***

    Do I look forward to Christ's return? Do I know that we will be judged and rewarded for doing well in goodness, faithfulness, and service to God and others? Do I feel the pull of the kingdom of God in my life?

I'm not suggesting that every one of the world's problems will be solved if we can answer these questions according to the implications I've written into them. I will say, however, that authentic answers along these lines go a long way in producing a healthy life and relationship with God. And this is where we're going in the rest of the book.

From this point on in the text, we won't see many more references to 'the forest,' 'the maps,' and 'the path.' These images have helped us to see the concepts behind Christianity. But if Christianity remains a concept, then there will be no real impact in our lives. If Jesus Christ is real and faith is a true experience, then it's time to move beyond the images.

Before We Break Camp

Great Wonders Daily

GOD CREATES PEOPLE

*** Incredible pics from Day 6 *** God overheard, "This is so good." ***

Garden of Eden— After creating airborne and aquatic animals. God continued to display his mastery over the physical sciences this morning by creating land animals. The highlight of the day came later when God created a man, after deciding to do so in his own likeness. God and the man, named Adam, spent quite awhile together, as the man was allowed to give names to all the animals.

As evening came, God caused Adam to fall asleep. God took one of his ribs and formed it into a woman — to be a helper and mate. A spokesman for God said that he and his favorite couple are enjoying themselves completely, and that God is now ready for a day off.

Full Story

—Genesis, chapters 1 & 2

Exhibit Opens Today

1st Quarter Earnings Much Higher Than Expected

7 ❧ God Creates People

Animals gather as Creator God kneels in the dirt.
He reaches down and presses his palm to the ground
—a perfect hand on the rich, fresh soil created just days ago.

A thought crosses his mind:
'Once he is formed and begins to breathe, a chain reaction will begin.'
Radio waves crackle as human history races through the Creator's thoughts.
Forbidden fruit. A brother murdered.
Villains and victims. Heroes and heretics. Suffering and heartache pound.
Yesterday's ... today's ... tomorrow's tragedies.

A drop falls as a perfect hand grabs the earth; sweat or emotion?
Flashes of Christ crucified. Thunder responds.
The sky trembles at the thought of the price—His only begotten Son?

He could brush his hands clean and walk away,
But the decision is ... love.

A perfect hand opens to reveal a perfect human body.

Okay, so actually it happened this way:

²⁶Then God said, "Let us make man in Our image, according to Our likeness; and let them rule over the fish of the sea and over the birds of the sky and over the cattle and over all the earth, and over every creeping thing that creeps on the earth." ²⁷God created man in His own image, in the image of God He created him; male and female He created them.

Genesis 1:26-27

⁷Then the LORD God formed man of dust from the ground, and breathed into his nostrils the breath of life; and man became a living being.

Genesis 2:7

"And now the news ..."

As the 20th Century drew to a close, there seemed to be a rush to categorize and organize our past 100 years—as if we wanted to leave the decades in better shape than we found them. Every day, during the final months and weeks of 1999, it seemed as if yet another list or ranking was published: from *Most Important Musical Works* and *Best World Literature*, to *Top Racehorses, Biggest Thinkers*, and *Favorite Mysteries*—even *Greatest Chinese Films*. One of the lists that caught my attention ranked the top news stories of the century[1]. Their sources generally agree on the events, if not the order.

- *Wright Brothers Fly at Kitty Hawk*
- *Japan Bombs Pearl Harbor*
- *U.S. Drops Atomic Bomb*
- *JFK Assassinated in Dallas*
- *Man Walks on the Moon*

Each of these events was captured on film. And if we've seen the pictures, then I'm sure we can see the images of these events in our minds right now.

On the other hand, when we remember *Man Walks on the Moon*, not only do we see the pictures, but we hear the words, "That's one small step for ... man, one giant leap for mankind[2]."

In regard to the first headline in God's history with people, it's the words—more than pictures—that carry the real impact. I can almost hear them now in a static-y, Neil Armstrong-like transmission. "Let us make man ... *crackle* ... in our image, according ... *pop* ... to our likeness."

I don't believe God spoke these incredible words as if he was looking for something to do on a Friday afternoon. Just as Armstrong's first words from the surface of the moon answered a declaration made by President Kennedy almost seven years earlier—"We choose to go to the moon in this decade, and the other things, not because they are easy, but because they are hard[3]."—I believe that God's words to make people in his own image also answered plans and preparations that came beforehand. Remember?

The kingdom of God has been the determining factor in all of his decisions from even before he said, "Let us make man in our image." If we were to see God's home movies of the moment he spoke those words, and we looked closely at what's in the background of the shot, we would see that God was standing in front of his kingdom.

These few words from God are not an off-the-cuff mumble, like "I think I'll watch the news." Rather, a climactic announcement which anticipates the arrival of friends—"I'm ready. Let's invite them in." Because these words are weightier than we may have thought, it's certainly worth it to delve deeper behind the headline.

> God's words to make people in his own image answered plans that came beforehand.

We've 'flown over the forest' and 'spent time learning the maps.' Now, as the adventure begins, we're standing here in the Garden of Eden, the site of the first great wonder. We're here to investigate the headline *God Creates People*.

Here's a crazy thought. What if the Garden of Eden was an international landmark that they were able to open up as a tourist attraction? I would guess that there are about a million-billion questions we would want to ask our tour guide as he or she led us through the exhibit. *Which came first; the chicken or the egg? What about dinosaurs? Is there life elsewhere in the universe? Did God create people to be sinfully flawed? What is 'conscience' made of?* I'm sure we could each add our own question or two to the list.

I've picked two questions for us to address in this chapter, and I'm almost sure that they're not the first ones to pop into anyone's mind. But they are important.

1. What does the phrase *the image of God* mean?
2. What can we learn from Adam's friendship with God?

We're looking at these specific questions because of our mission statement (as you wonder when exactly I outlined our mission statement). We're here "to seek truth regarding a relationship with God, by studying God's history with people." We'll have to talk chickens and eggs another day because right now we're following the story of a lifetime.

"What does the phrase *the image of God* mean?"

Traditional Christianity teaches that God is one God in three persons: the Father, the Son, and the Holy Spirit. This understanding of God is known as *the Trinity*. Each of the three persons is completely God, and the one God is the three persons.

The Trinity is perhaps the most difficult aspect of God's nature for people to comprehend. Maybe you've heard the Trinity defined in terms of one egg being the shell, the albumen (or 'the white'), and the yoke. You might have heard the analogies of one man being a son, a husband, and a father, or H_2O being ice, water, or steam. But even the teachers who use these analogies accept the fact that they fail to truly explain the Trinity.

Perhaps the truest explanation has been right under our noses since the very beginning. Human beings are a type of trinity. Each of us can be described as one person being a spirit, a soul, and a body. Each part of my person is me, yet I am made up of each part.

I've been aware of this comparison of the Trinity of God (capitol T) and the trinity of mankind (small t) for quite a number of years. But, honestly, it's never really satisfied me in regard to our question "What does *the image of God* mean?" As a matter of fact, I've since discovered that the idea of the Trinity barely scratches the surface, that there's something more, something truly amazing to be learned about the image of God.

I once gave a presentation called *When Man Sees God*. What I did was research the stories in the Bible which tell of people seeing God, either face-to-face or in a vision. And I shared with my audience exactly what God looks like. Unfortunately, my snapshots of God didn't really suggest 'an image' that people have in common with him. Look at the following example and I'm sure you'll understand what I mean.

God Appears to the Prophet Ezekiel

---

[26]*Now above the expanse that was over their heads there was something resembling a throne, like lapis lazuli in appearance; and on that which resembled a throne, high up, was a figure with* the appearance of a man. [27]*Then I noticed from the appearance of His loins and upward something like glowing metal that looked like fire all around within it, and from the appearance of His loins and downward I saw something like fire; and there was a radiance around Him.* [28]*As the appearance of the rainbow in the clouds on a rainy day, so was the appearance of the surrounding radiance. Such was the appearance*

of the likeness of the glory of the LORD. And when I saw it, I fell on my face and heard a voice speaking.   *Ezekiel 1:26-28*

Despite the underlined phrase, "the appearance of a man," I'm pretty sure that God's glorious appearance is *not* what the 'image of God' refers to.

Personally, I wish there were scriptures in which Adam described the physical features of the God who created him. *The LORD was full of vitality, standing 6'5". His fatherly eyes were seasoned with wisdom; his hands, active with a son's youth as a living radiance swirled around him.* But if there was such a description, maybe we would miss the truth behind God's image.

John opens his biography of Jesus by telling us that, although no one has seen God at any time, his only son—who is himself God, who is close to his Father's heart—has revealed God to us[4]. John also recorded what Jesus revealed about God, his image, and us:

[23]*"But an hour is coming, and now is, when the true worshipers will worship the Father in spirit and truth; for such people the Father seeks to be His worshipers.* [24]*God is spirit, and those who worship Him must worship in spirit and truth."*

John 4:23-24

I believe that a related meaning behind the words "those who worship him," could be "those who know him," "those who interact with him." God is spirit, and those people who desire to experience him must do so through their spirit. The human spirit is the image of God.

A Healthy Spirit Experiences ...

Describe one aspect of your body, your soul, and your spirit. For example, "My hair is curly." This is one of the questions I asked participants in the first few *8 Great Wonders* courses we held. And consistently, I saw that people found the idea of describing their spirit rather challenging.

It's important for Christians to *have* healthy spiritual experiences, so it's very important to know *what* a healthy spirit can experience.

We're going to identify about 35 different characteristics that can be experienced by a spirit that has been born again. The problem is, some of these spiritual experiences sound like those that anybody in the world can have, Christian or not.

- Christians can experience God's comfort (in their spirit); anyone can experience sympathy (in their soul).
- We can experience God's holiness (spirit); anyone can experience clean living (soul).
- The Holy Spirit can produce self-control in our spirit; anyone can work up will power in their mind.
- The Holy Spirit produces joy in life; anyone can be happy in the moment.
- Christians can experience God's gift of wisdom, but anyone can have intelligent thoughts.
- Christians speak in tongues; anyone can babble gibberish.
- Christian men and women have been called to be evangelists or teachers, yet many non-Christians can motivate or inspire others in a positive way.

Because of these similarities, we absolutely have to consider this question first. *Is there really a difference between 'spirit experiences' and 'soul experiences'?* After all, we saw in Chapter 5 that the spirit and soul can be described in terms that make us think of conjoined twins. Wouldn't that mean that the experiences are really the same?

Let's look at a statement made by Paul.

> [15]... *I will pray with the spirit and I will pray with the mind also; I will sing with the spirit and I will sing with the mind also.*   *1 Corinthians 14:15*

See the word *also*? Paul is talking about two kinds of prayer, two kinds of singing—"in the spirit" and "with the mind." In the same passage, he says that "my spirit prays, but my mind is unfruitful." There *are* spirit experiences, and from what I've seen, they're fuller, longer-lasting, and more deeply impacting than soul experiences.

Spiritual experiences seem to suggest a life lived a step or two above normal.

"Grace to you and peace from God our Father and the Lord Jesus Christ." This greeting appears in almost every book of the New Testament between the Gospels and Revelation. We see from this statement, and many other scriptures, that the experiences of a healthy spirit, like grace and peace, come from God. What we've been calling *soul experiences* are all self-initiated. Anyone can experience clean living and will power. With a few candles, soft music, and aroma therapy, anyone can experience calmness. But only God's people can feel the depths of the peace that comes from him.

> [7]*And the peace of God, which surpasses all comprehension, will guard your hearts and your minds in Christ Jesus.*   *Philippians 4:7*

I've experienced God's peace when circumstances demanded that I panic—heart pounding, knees knocking. Peace doesn't make sense at a time like that. But in those anxious moments, I've been able to think straight and make right decisions. While most people can enjoy calmness in a calm atmosphere, Christians can enjoy God's peace in any atmosphere.

I mentioned that we're looking at about 35 characteristics from God that Christians can experience. There are many more than 35 different kinds of healthy spiritual experiences. There are several areas that won't be covered in this section; like God's character traits and his promises to his children. These would be great places for someone to begin their own research. But what I do want to talk about are areas that indicate that a healthy human spirit actually develops over time.

Whenever I think about the different stages we go through during our lifetime, whether it's physically, emotionally or spiritually, an album title comes to mind: *Birth, School, Work, Death*. It was recorded by GODFATHERS, a British punk band from the late 1980s. On the surface, the title implies a wasted, empty life; which certainly fits the angst of punk rock. But, call me crazy, I see something meaningful and purposeful in those four words.

... Birth

What an incredible time it was—the birth of our daughter. Friends wrapped the front door of our house like a baby gift. Our answering machine was filled with "welcome to the world" messages. It seemed that everyone and their mother stopped by to see our 7 pound, 13 ounce miracle of life, who, in turn, seemed to fill us all with the hope and promise of a better tomorrow. She was fresh and new and beautiful. She was perfect.

Can we see similar images in these initial spirit experiences?

- The Holy Spirit
- Mercy and Forgiveness
- Reconciliation
- Righteousness
- Eternal life

Have you ever heard a new Christian say anything like this? "I was overwhelmed with a sense of God's love." "My guilt and shame just melted, like the weight of the world had lifted from my shoulders." "My addiction was instantly broken. God made me new again." "I felt God's presence. I cried for the first time in forever."

There are people who can vividly remember a time like this in their life. And some may even have the initial love and acceptance of a church family in their life's history as well. But if mature Christians neglect to raise the 'new baby,' then it's not likely that normal development will take place afterwards.

... School

[**Warning:**] *[12]For though by this time you ought to be teachers, you have need again for someone to teach you the elementary principles of the oracles of God, and you have come to need milk and not solid food. [13]For everyone who partakes only of milk is not accustomed to the word of righteousness, for he is an infant. [14]But solid food is for the mature, who because of practice have their senses trained to discern good and evil.*   Hebrews 5:12-14 [warning added]

There are two primary elements in any setting where education takes place; the teacher and the student. From where the student sits, information is given so that a test can be passed. But from the teacher's perspective, lessons are taught so that skills and abilities can be identified and developed.

We may think that the Bible and church are merely sources of information, barely more than facts and figures which seem irrelevant today. But it's the Holy Spirit's job to raise God's children. His intention is not to fill our heads with knowledge only, but to prepare us to be God's hands and feet wherever we are. Whether indirectly, through the Bible and prayer, or directly, the Holy Spirit initiates the following experiences in our lives to identify who we are and to prepare us for the work we're meant to do.

- Grace
- Encouragement
- Comfort
- Revelation
- Understanding
- Knowledge of God's Will
- Power

If, as a student, we accept the Holy Spirit's work in our lives the way an athlete accepts his or her daily practice drills, then we will come to know the gifts and talents that God has put inside us. We'll choose to appreciate and develop them, knowing all along that God will use them for his purposes.

As maturity is taking place, the unseen spirit inside us will continually express itself in the following attitudes and actions. They're called 'the fruit of the (Holy) Spirit:'

- Love
- Joy
- Peace
- Patience
- Kindness
- Goodness
- Faithfulness
- Gentleness
- Self-control

... Work

Depending on the culture, a person may become an apprentice or an intern as a teenager or a young adult. With this in mind, it might seem that "doing the work of the ministry" is something that happens only after years and years of growth as a Christian. That's not really the case. A better analogy would be that of *Bring Your Child to Work Day*, which we loosely observe in America.

My daughter was only five when she came to work with me the first time. She distributed mail to my co-workers, put small boxes on the weight scale, dropped overnight packages in the bin downstairs, and dialed the telephone numbers of several vendors for me.

Now, did she do the work that day, or did I do the work through her? As the Holy Spirit leads our lives, we find ourselves in the same position as my young daughter—tagging along as God does the work 'through us.'

Paul told us that there are various gifts, ministries, and effects, but it's the same Holy Spirit who works through each of these things. And he said that the manifestation of the Spirit is given to each one for the common good[5].

These gifts are:

- Words of Wisdom
- Words of Knowledge
- Faith
- Gifts of Healing

- Miracles
- Prophecy
- Discernment
- Speaking in tongues
- Interpretation of tongues

These 'gifts of the Spirit' may sound like strange experiences, but remember, Christians are meant to live life on God's terms. Believe me; we *want* everything God has for us. While I would be surprised if there was a Christian who has experienced all of these gifts, because of the verse above I would find it more difficult to believe there was a maturing Christian who didn't experience any of them.

In addition to the gifts of the Holy Spirit, some of us will experience God's call to ministry service. Those who served God as Prophets and Apostles in the Bible did so because he called them to do it. From Ephesians 4:11, we know that when people serve as apostles, prophets, evangelists, pastors, or teachers, that they do their work so that we're better equipped to do ours.

... Death

With the new birth of our spirit came eternal life. So how in the world can we include 'death' in the development of a healthy human spirit?

Paul contrasted this world and the world to come. He looked at our lives here and now and said, "When I was a child, I spoke like a child, thought like a child, reasoned like a child." Then he lifted his face toward the sky and said, "When I became a man, I did away with childish things[6]."

> [8]*... but if there are gifts of prophecy, they will be done away; if there are tongues, they will cease; if there is knowledge, it will be done away. [9]For we know in part and we prophesy in part; [10]but when the perfect comes, the partial will be done away.*   1 Corinthians 13:8-10

Death, so to speak, will come to some of the things God uses to develop and grow us up. But, thankfully, *"Faith, hope and love go on forever[7]."*

It's important for us to keep an eye on these spiritual experiences, using them as gauges to see whether or not God is active in our life, whether or not our friendship with him is growing. But let's never lose sight of the eternal characteristics. How are we doing in regard to faith, hope, and love?

The fact that people were created in the image of God certainly carries implications with it. I'm sure we've seen them in the characteristics that a healthy human spirit can experience. But for what reason does God want it to be this way? I wonder if there's anything we can learn from Adam, the first person to ever experience faith, hope, and love perfectly.

☙ Genesis 2:8-9 and Genesis 2:15-22 give us some specific information about the friendship between God and Adam. Read the passage. Identify and <u>underline</u> the following:

1. God provided Adam's home.
2. God gave Adam a purpose.
3. God set Adam's boundaries.
4. God made Adam's mate and brought her to him.

⁸The LORD God planted a garden toward the east, in Eden; and there He placed the man whom He had formed. ⁹Out of the ground the LORD God caused to grow every tree that is pleasing to the sight and good for food; the tree of life also in the midst of the garden, and the tree of the knowledge of good and evil.

Genesis 2:8-9

the story concludes …

¹⁵Then the LORD God took the man and put him into the garden of Eden to cultivate it and keep it. ¹⁶The LORD God commanded the man, saying, "From any tree of the garden you may eat freely; ¹⁷but from the tree of the knowledge of good and evil you shall not eat, for in the day that you eat from it you will surely die."

¹⁸Then the LORD God said, "It is not good for the man to be alone; I will make him a helper suitable for him." ¹⁹Out of the ground the LORD God formed every beast of the field and every bird of the sky, and brought them to the man to see what he would call them; and whatever the man called a living creature, that was its name. ²⁰The man gave names to all the cattle, and to the birds of the sky, and to every beast of the field, but for Adam there was not found a helper suitable for him. ²¹So the LORD God caused a deep sleep to fall upon the man, and he slept; then He took one of his ribs and closed up the flesh at that place. ²²The LORD God fashioned into a woman the rib which He had taken from the man, and brought her to the man.

Genesis 2:15-22

There's a clever song called *Man Gave Names to All the Animals* on one of my favorite Bob Dylan albums, *Slow Train Coming*. The song is based on a couple of verses from the passage we just read. I want us to focus a few more moments here.

> [19]*Out of the ground the LORD God formed every beast of the field and every bird of the sky, and brought them to the man to see what he would call them; and whatever the man called a living creature, that was its name.* [20]*The man gave names to all the cattle, and to the birds of the sky, and to every beast of the field, ...*
>
> *Genesis 2:19-20a*

☙ In this 'scene,' what might it have been like if God and Adam had been:

Two scientists

Boss and employee

A couple of friends

☙ Which of these relationships might describe the feelings you have regarding your relationship with God? Share your reasons why.

Although there are many individual scriptures that refer to Creation, there are only three places in the Bible where full chapters reveal the details.

- Genesis 1
- Job 38-41 (Job rhymes with *robe*)
- Psalm 104

The first chapter of Genesis is very organized and structured. Quite honestly, it reads like a scientist's personal journal. *On the first day; this category. On the second day; that category. On the third day ... fourth day ... fifth ... sixth ...*

The four chapters in Job read something like an official reprimand; the kind we might find in an employee's personnel file. *Where were you when I did this? Where were you when I did that?*

Yes, sir. You're the boss, and I'm not.

But the Psalm—now that's another story. The 104th Psalm takes the facts in Genesis and offers them to the Sovereign King in Job from a position of praise and thankfulness.

There was a husband and wife who attended one of our *8 Great Wonders* courses. She was analytical to the nth degree. He had been brought up in an extremely strict traditional church.

I asked them, "Which of these relationships best describes your feelings about your relationship with God: two scientists, boss and employee, or a couple of friends?"

Without hesitation, she answered, "Scientists. Just give me the facts, God. Just tell me what to do."

I was caught off guard by her rapid-fire answer and didn't know how to respond, so I quickly turned to her husband. "How would you answer this question?"

He said slowly, "Boss and employee. I've always thought that God was angry with me. I figure he would have fired me if he could."

I didn't know what to say. Naively, I thought that everyone would answer "a couple of friends," even if they didn't really believe it. But this couple was honest and sincere. They were being real.

The Holy Spirit spoke to my heart, so I turned to the wife. "Do you think scientists might take a coffee break every now and then?"

"Sure."

"I don't mean to presume to talk for God, but I think he wants you to know that it's okay to remove the lab coat and hang out with him in the break room every once in awhile."

She smiled. "I would like that."

I looked at her husband. "I don't know that people do it as much these days as they used to, but how would you feel about inviting your boss, God, home for dinner; just to get to know each other? There's a verse in the Bible that says that he wants to share a meal with us as friends[8]."

Looking up, he also smiled and nodded.

Personally, I think there are three important questions that we should be asking about our relationship with God.

1. Have I accepted the information in Genesis as fact?
2. Have I learned the lesson of Job; that the facts put God in his rightful place and me in mine, that God is the Sovereign and I am the servant?
3. Have I bowed, like the psalmist, to the wonderful God who is responsible for the facts?

Here's another way of looking at it. What if, in our relationship with God, we experience the 'cooperative effort' between scientists, the 'responsible authority' between boss and employee, *and* the 'love and respect' between friends? Couldn't we be describing the relationship between a good father and his child? And wouldn't this understanding help us in our acts of worship?

Worship comes easier as we get to know God better, as we experience more of him. So let's offer him our cooperation, as we submit to his authority, and live in his love.

John wrote that love isn't defined by our love for God, but by his love for us *first*[9]. As we experience God's love, as well as the other qualities that we've looked at, we'll find ourselves offering God the worship that he seeks more and more. And we'll also be able to help others move from the facts, to the right perspective, to becoming true worshippers of God.

The Extra Effort (Search & Rescue)

😕 *God Creates People*—Why does it matter? Taken at face value, what implications does this headline have for the entire human race? ***Important:*** *Your notes here will be used in an exercise later in the book.*

😕 *God Creates People*—What difference does it make for you? Think about these statements and summarize your response below.

- I believe that people are built to experience friendship with God.
- I can take God at his word.
- I know my place before him.
- I am the kind of worshipper he is seeking.

* * *

😕 If you can, note a recent news story, as well as a personal story, that relates to topics in this chapter.

News:

Personal:

ᐓ List two things that impacted you as you read the chapter or participated in a
   group discussion.

_____

_____

_____

Scoring for *Search & Rescue* discussion groups:

   Read-4 ∗ Notes-8 ∗ News-1 ∗ Personal-2 ∗ Impact-16 ∗ Total-_____

[1] Newseum—The Interactive Museum of News: www.Newseum.org

[2] These words were spoken by Neil Armstrong on July 20th, 1969, from the surface of the moon.

[3] These words were spoken by President John F. Kennedy on September 12th, 1962, during a speech in Houston, Texas.

[4] John 1:18

[5] 1 Corinthians 12:5-7

[6] 1 Corinthians 13:11

[7] 1 Corinthians 13:13

[8] Revelation 3:20

[9] 1 John 4:10

PEOPLE SIN AGAINST GOD

*** Choice has devastating consequences *** Garden off-limits, Is God leaving? ***

East of Eden – Details are sketchy, but something seems to have gone very wrong in paradise. The Garden of Eden was shut down this afternoon as God met with Adam, Eve and a serpent behind closed doors. A short while later Adam and his wife were escorted out of the garden. A heavily armed angel has since been seen standing guard at the garden's entrance. The distraught couple has now gone into seclusion, but reporters were able to speak with them briefly some time earlier. Adam reportedly commented, "God gave her to me, and then she tricked me." At that point, Eve is said to have responded sharply, "Sure I did it, but I'm the victim here." The serpent has not been seen since the meeting with God. God's spokesman said that, "at least for the time being, he's not talking to any of you."

Full Story
—Genesis, Chapter 3

Runner Thrown Out at Home, Manager Explodes

Edwards Retires After Defeat

8 ❧ People Sin Against God

One Moment Minus God

*¹Now the serpent was more crafty than any beast of the field which the
LORD God had made. And he said to the woman, "Indeed, has God said, 'You
shall not eat from any tree of the garden'?" ²The woman said to the serpent,
"From the fruit of the trees of the garden we may eat; ³but from the fruit of the
tree which is in the middle of the garden, God has said, 'You shall not eat from it
or touch it, or you will die.'" ⁴The serpent said to the woman, "You surely will
not die! ⁵For God knows that in the day you eat from it your eyes will be opened,
and you will be like God, knowing good and evil." ⁶When the woman saw that
the tree was good for food, and that it was a delight to the eyes, and that the tree
was desirable to make one wise, she took from its fruit and ate; and she gave
also to her husband with her, and he ate. ⁷Then the eyes of both of them were
opened, and they knew that they were naked; and they sewed fig leaves
together and made themselves loin coverings.* Genesis 3:1-7

It's not a part of the Bible's inspired scriptures, but the Book of Jubilees[1],
written about 100 to 150 BC, states that Adam and Eve lived seven years before
they sinned against God. We certainly cannot regard the information in the Book

of Jubilees as being equal to that which is found in the Bible; however, this little tidbit does present some interesting food for thought. What might it have been like to have had a perfectly loving, on-going friendship with God, as well as a beautifully harmonious marriage, for that length of time? If we can even begin to grasp the wonderfulness of those relationships, then maybe we can also begin to understand the devastating sense of loss that followed.

⁸They heard the sound of the LORD God walking in the garden in the cool of the day, and the man and his wife hid themselves from the presence of the LORD God among the trees of the garden. ⁹Then the LORD God called to the man, and said to him, "Where are you?" ¹⁰He said, "I heard the sound of You in the garden, and I was afraid because I was naked; so I hid myself." ¹¹And He said, "Who told you that you were naked? Have you eaten from the tree of which I commanded you not to eat?" ¹²The man said, "The woman whom You gave to be with me, she gave me from the tree, and I ate." ¹³Then the LORD God said to the woman, "What is this you have done?" And the woman said, "The serpent deceived me, and I ate." ¹⁴The LORD God said to the serpent,

> *"Because you have done this,*
> *Cursed are you more than all cattle,*
> *And more than every beast of the field;*
> *On your belly you will go,*
> *And dust you will eat*
> *All the days of your life;*
> *¹⁵And I will put enmity*
> *Between you and the woman,*
> *And between your seed and her seed;*
> *He shall bruise you on the head,*
> *And you shall bruise him on the heel."*

¹⁶To the woman He said,

> *"I will greatly multiply*
> *Your pain in childbirth,*
> *In pain you will bring forth children;*
> *Yet your desire will be for your husband,*
> *And he will rule over you."*

¹⁷Then to Adam He said, "Because you have listened to the voice of your wife, and have eaten from the tree about which I commanded you, saying, 'You shall not eat from it';

> *Cursed is the ground because of you;*
> *In toil you will eat of it*

All the days of your life.

¹⁸Both thorns and thistles it shall grow for you;

And you will eat the plants of the field;

¹⁹By the sweat of your face

You will eat bread,

Till you return to the ground,

Because from it you were taken;

For you are dust,

And to dust you shall return."

²⁰Now the man called his wife's name Eve, because she was the mother of all the living. ²¹The LORD God made garments of skin for Adam and his wife, and clothed them.

²²Then the LORD God said, "Behold, the man has become like one of Us, knowing good and evil; and now, he might stretch out his hand, and take also from the tree of life, and eat, and live forever"— ²³therefore the LORD God sent him out from the garden of Eden, to cultivate the ground from which he was taken. ²⁴So He drove the man out; and at the east of the garden of Eden He stationed the cherubim and the flaming sword which turned every direction to guard the way to the tree of life.

Genesis 3:8-24

It's sad to me that Adam lived to be 930 years old, yet after he and Eve sinned, there are no more stories in the Bible indicating an on-going friendship with God. The next mention of Adam's name in the Bible is found as a physically and emotionally-stricken Job is declaring his innocence to God.

"Have I covered up my sins like Adam, by hiding them²?"

Almost everyone throughout history knows what Adam did. That's a legacy I wouldn't wish on anyone.

The Legacy of Adam

¹²... through one man sin entered into the world, and death through sin, and so death spread to all men ...

Romans 5:12

Something more than just sin and death may have spread from Adam to the rest of us. God said that Adam and Eve possessed 'the knowledge of good and evil' after they disobeyed him. Could this knowledge be something that has been passed on to each of us as well?

Early in the development of the *8 Great Wonders* material, I thought I came up with an absolutely fantastic discussion question. *In your opinion, is the knowledge of good and evil the same as knowing right from wrong?* (Think a moment about how you would answer the question.) I thought I knew the answer and I was convinced that everyone would respond the same way. But, having discussed the question with several groups, I've found that opinions are pretty much divided 50/50 between yes and no and that dozens of different reasons can be given to support each view.

Here's why I asked the question in the first place.

When God came to Adam and Eve right after their sin, he asked, "Who told you that you were naked?" But just four verses prior to his question we see that no one told them they were naked.

> *7... the eyes of both of them were opened, and they knew that they were naked; and they sewed fig leaves together ...*
>
> *Genesis 3:7*

If God knows everything—and that's what the Bible teaches—then why would he ask, "Who told you?" when a question that's more to the point would have been, "Did you eat from the forbidden tree?"

Here's something to consider. In the last chapter we saw that God was the source of everything for Adam and Eve: their home, their purpose, their boundaries, and their spouse. God was the initiator in the relationship; Adam and Eve were responders. God's question, "Who told you?" could have reminded Adam that he was made to respond. And God's question might have suggested something else. "Adam, who's *going to* tell you ... now that we're separated?"

Unfortunately, Adam's only answer would have been, "No one. I'll decide for myself what's good and what's evil."

Whatever it really is, I believe that we all have the knowledge of good and evil that Adam and Eve gained. We've got it, our children have it, and they'll pass it on to our grandchildren as well. And I believe this because our natural thought tends to be that we don't need anyone to tell us what's right and what's wrong. *I can do this life thing on my own.*

Look at how the "I don't need anyone" mindset played out in the first generations that followed Adam. Could these be snapshots of humanity today?

True or false? *The knowledge of good and evil gives us the ability to decide for ourselves what's right and what's wrong. And it means that all of our decisions are correct.*

Adam and Eve's Son Cain

> *6Then the LORD said to Cain, "Why are you angry? And why has your countenance fallen? 7If you do well, will not your countenance be lifted up? And if you do not do well, sin is crouching at the door; and its desire is for you, but*

you must master it." ⁸Cain told Abel his brother. And it came about when they were in the field, that Cain rose up against Abel his brother and killed him.

Genesis 4:6-8

The People of Noah's Generation

⁵Then the LORD saw that the wickedness of man was great on the earth, and that every intent of the thoughts of his heart was only evil continually. ⁶The LORD was sorry that He had made man on the earth, and He was grieved in His heart. ⁷The LORD said, "I will blot out man whom I have created from the face of the land, from man to animals to creeping things and to birds of the sky; for I am sorry that I have made them."

Genesis 6:5-7

The Citizens of Sodom and Gomorrah

²⁰And the LORD said, "The outcry of Sodom and Gomorrah is indeed great, and their sin is exceedingly grave. ²¹I will go down now, and see if they have done entirely according to its outcry, which has come to Me; and if not, I will know."

Genesis 18:20-21

the story continues ...

²³Abraham came near and said, "Will You indeed sweep away the righteous with the wicked? ²⁴Suppose there are fifty righteous within the city; will You indeed sweep it away and not spare the place for the sake of the fifty righteous who are in it? ²⁵Far be it from You to do such a thing, to slay the righteous with the wicked, so that the righteous and the wicked are treated alike. Far be it from You! Shall not the Judge of all the earth deal justly?" ²⁶So the LORD said, "If I find in Sodom fifty righteous within the city, then I will spare the whole place on their account."

Genesis 18:23-26

the story continues ...

³²Then he said, "Oh may the Lord not be angry, and I shall speak only this once; suppose ten are found there?" And He said, "I will not destroy it on account of the ten."

Genesis 18:32

the story concludes ...

²⁴Then the LORD rained on Sodom and Gomorrah brimstone and fire from the LORD out of heaven, ²⁵and He overthrew those cities, and all the valley, and all the inhabitants of the cities, and what grew on the ground.

Genesis 19:24-25

NOTES

I believe that the lives of Cain, the people of Noah's generation, and the citizens of Sodom and Gomorrah were disasters because they refused to learn from Eve. *Those who do not learn from history are doomed to repeat it*[3].

There's a common thread running through the stories of all these people. It's implied in several phrases from the Bible.

- Regarding Cain—"Sin is crouching at the door; and its desire is for you, but you must master it."
- Regarding Noah's generation—"Every intent of the thoughts of [man's] heart was only evil continually."
- Regarding the people of Sodom and Gomorrah—"Their sin is exceedingly grave."

While the words *sin* and *evil* are obvious in these phrases, the implication behind these words seems to be hiding. Where there's sin and evil, there's temptation. And where there's temptation, there hides in the shadows a tempter.

We have an enemy. And I'm not just motioning towards Christians when I say that. The entire human race has an enemy. The Bible refers to him as "the great dragon ... the serpent of old who is called the devil and Satan, who deceives the whole world[4]."

Jesus said that Satan is a thief who comes only to steal, kill and destroy[5]. Elsewhere in the Bible, he is compared to a roaring lion, prowling around and looking for someone to devour[6].

While we should take these descriptions seriously, there's no reason for us to picture a menacing red man with horns and a tail. Satan's greatest advantage isn't a threatening physical appearance, but the fact that we don't see him at all when he's tempting us. But maybe we should. The prophet Isaiah was referring to him when he made the following proclamation:

> [16]*Those who see you will gaze at you,*
> *They will ponder over you, saying,*
> *"Is this the man who made the earth tremble,*
> *Who shook kingdoms,*
> [17]*Who made the world like a wilderness*
> *And overthrew its cities,*
> *Who did not allow his prisoners to go home?"*
>
> *Isaiah 14:16-17*

Or in other words, "Him? You've got to be kidding!"

As long as Satan remains 'invisible,' as long as he goes unrecognized as the source of temptation to sin, we will continue to blame others, ourselves, and even God for our struggles in life.

Paul understood that our battles *aren't* with people—they aren't even with God—but with "spiritual forces of wickedness[7]." That's why he wrote, "We don't want to be taken advantage of by him, so we aren't ignorant of Satan's schemes[8]." Let's shine a light at the shadows Satan likes to hide in. Let's expose his schemes.

There are three aspects of Satan's character that we can absolutely count on. The first is the fact that he appeals to something he knows we all have lurking on the inside of us.

> [16]*For all that is in the world, ₐ**the lust of the flesh** and ᵦ**the lust of the eyes** and ᵧ**the boastful pride of life**, is not from the Father, but is from the world.*
>
> 1 John 2:16 [emphasis added]

Jesus called Satan "the ruler of this world[9]." So "the world" in the verse above is referring to philosophies and ways of life that are inspired by Satan.

Now, let's take another look at the highlighted phrases in the verse above, and then compare them to the ones in the scriptures below.

The Temptation of Eve
_____

[6]*When the woman saw that the tree was ₐ**good for food**, and that it was ᵦ**a delight to the eyes**, and that the tree was ᵧ**desirable to make one wise**, she took from its fruit and ate; and she gave also to her husband with her, and he ate.*
Genesis 3:6 [emphasis added]
_____

The scripture that follows is the first of many Old Testament prophecies that speak of someone coming in history who would undo the damage that the serpent caused in the Garden of Eden.

> [15]*"And I will put enmity*
> *Between you and the woman,*
> *And between your seed and her seed;*
> *He shall bruise you on the head,*
> *And you shall bruise him on the heel."*
>
> Genesis 3:15

And 1 John 3:8 is one of many New Testament scriptures that reveal the identity of that "coming someone."

8... the devil has sinned from the beginning. The Son of God appeared for this purpose, to destroy the works of the devil.

1 John 3:8

Jesus Christ is the "seed" of Eve, whose heel was bruised (crucifixion) when he bruised the serpent's head (breaking our slavery to sin).

Just as we have the written record of Eve's temptation in Genesis, we also have the written record of how "her seed" encountered temptation, in the Gospels of Matthew and Luke[10]. Remember; the tempter who came to both Eve and Jesus is the same one who tempts us today. Let's pay close attention to the following highlighted phrases. We'll compare them to those we've already seen.

The Temptation of Eve's Seed—Jesus

*3And the devil said to Him, "If You are the Son of God, ₐ**tell this stone to become bread."** ...*

*5And he led Him up and ᵦ**showed Him all the kingdoms of the world** in a moment of time. 6And the devil said to Him, "I will give You all this domain and its glory; for it has been handed over to me, and I give it to whomever I wish. 7Therefore if You worship before me, it shall all be Yours." ...*

9And he led Him to Jerusalem and had Him stand on the pinnacle of the temple, and said to Him, "If You are the Son of God, throw Yourself down from here; 10for it is written,

*'ᵪ**He will command His angels concerning You to guard You,'***
11and,

'On their hands they will bear You up,
So that You will not strike Your foot against a stone.'"

Luke 4:3, 5-7 & 9-11 [emphasis added]

While actually writing this chapter, I smiled as one of the radio preachers was teaching the following concept. I remembered how my dad taught it when I was growing up.

Here's the sum of what both men taught.

a. "Good for food," from Eve's temptation, and "tell this stone to become bread," from Jesus' temptation, are both statements that capture the attention of "the lust of the flesh."

b.   "A delight to the eyes" (Eve) and "showed Him all the kingdoms of the world" (Jesus) are enticing to "the lust of the eyes."

c.   "Desirable to make one wise" (Eve) and "He will command his angels concerning you to guard you" (Jesus) cause us to fantasize about "the boastful pride of life." (After all, how cool would it be to be as wise as God, or to have an angel catch you and escort you wherever you go?)

Satan tempts us through "the lust of the flesh," "the lust of the eyes," and "the boastful pride of life." We can bank on the fact that he will try to capture our attention, enticing something deep within us, trying to get us to think about something sinful and harmful longer than we should. We can bank on it because he's betting that, due to our independent nature, we'll decide for ourselves what's good and what's evil.

There's a second aspect of Satan's character that we can be absolutely convinced about. It's the fact that everything he says is a lie.

Jesus told us that Satan "does not stand in the truth because there is no truth in him. Whenever he speaks a lie, he speaks from his own nature, for he is a liar and the father of lies[11]." If someone could say it any clearer than that, I'd be amazed.

The serpent had said to Eve, confidently, "You will not die," but the very day she and Adam sinned they lost everything they had known; their perfect friendship with God, their harmonious marriage to one another, and their paradise home. Sin and death came into the world that day[12]. The serpent definitely lied!

> Satan is a proven liar. He promises outcomes that don't happen and offers to give us things that aren't his to give.

When Satan told Jesus "I will give you all this domain and its glory; for it has been handed over to me, and I give it to whomever I wish," he was lying. We know this for sure because, in his final words before ascending into heaven, Jesus said, "All authority has been given to me in heaven and on earth[13]." It was God who gave Jesus this "domain," not Satan. Jesus also said, "I was dead, and behold, I am alive forevermore, and I have the keys of death and of Hades[14]" (another name for hell). That puts to rest a common misconception. It means that Satan doesn't even hold the deed to hell.

There's quite a bit more we could talk about in regard to Satan being a liar, but the fact is, there's no such thing as a lie unless there's also something called *the truth*. And that brings us to the third aspect of Satan's character; he always challenges what God says.

A friend of mine picked me up to join him on a research trip. He neglected to tell me where we were going until we pulled up in front of an occult bookstore. I did what any true-blue Christian would do; I whispered prayers and hummed hymns the whole time we were inside.

As I looked around at the books on the various shelves I noticed something: The books on Eastern Mysticism were next to the Satanism section, which was next to the New Age material, which was beside the handbooks regarding Wicca practices.

I looked over at the clerk behind the counter, who was busy charting a woman's horoscope. *These religions contradict each other. Doesn't he care which one his customers embrace?*

Then it dawned on me: *No. Satan doesn't care which path a person picks, as long as it isn't God's path of truth.*

Most of us would be totally put off by Death Metal music and an appetite for the gruesome. So Satan offers us something other than Satanism. And it really doesn't matter what he offers us, just as long as it keeps us from a personal friendship with our Creator. It doesn't even have to be a 'religion.' Our enemy tries to keep us from God with all sorts of things—from alcohol, drugs, and illicit sex, to sports, gardening, and television. Just about anything can keep us from fulfilling what Jesus called "the greatest commandment": to "love the Lord God with all of our heart, soul, mind, and strength[15]." Seems hard to believe, but even the second commandment—to "love our neighbor as ourselves[16]"—can keep us from God if it's our top priority instead.

Satan has a broad arsenal of lies when it comes to the human race at large, but when an individual gets too close to this "salvation through Jesus" business, this "relationship with God" thing, Satan zeroes in on a single primary target; God's Word—the Bible.

God's Word! Attack!

Before any mention of a tempter in the Bible, God told Adam that there was an 'or else' in regard to disobedience. *You will surely die[17]*. I don't think it was a coincidence that the serpent challenged God's words with similar words of his own. *You surely will not die[18]*. He did the same thing when he tempted Jesus.

> [6]*and* [the devil] *said to Him, "If You are the Son of God, throw Yourself down; for it is written,*
>
> *'He will command His angels concerning You';*
> *and*
>
> *'On their hands they will bear You up,*
> *So that You will not strike Your foot against a stone.'"*   Matthew 4:6

Despite what it may look like, Satan wasn't actually quoting scripture. Here's the passage as it appears in the Book of Psalms.

> [11]*For He will give His angels charge concerning you,*
> **To guard you in all your ways.**
> [12]*They will bear you up in their hands,*
> *That you do not strike your foot against a stone.*
> [13]**You will tread upon the lion and cobra,**
> **The young lion and the serpent you will trample down.**
>
> *Psalm 91:11-13* [emphasis added]

Satan was very careful, wasn't he? The implication behind "to guard you in all your ways" is that *your ways* are righteous. Satan wouldn't have wanted to remind Jesus of this, so he left it out. And then there's that phrase "the serpent you will trample down." Satan definitely wouldn't have wanted Jesus hearing these words, so he stopped short.

Satan doesn't quote scripture; he twists it. He denies God's authority as he entices us through our knowledge of good and evil. He contradicts God's truth with every lie he whispers to us. He challenges God's faithfulness to deliver on the promises he has spoken to us, about us, or for our well-being. We can expect Satan to use these schemes against us.

But maybe there's something that Satan should come to expect from us in return. After all, we can respond to Satan's lies the same way Jesus did. Maybe Satan should expect us to respond to him with the Word of God as well.

- [4]*And Jesus answered him, "It is written* (Deuteronomy 8:3)*, 'Man shall not live on bread alone.' "*   Luke 4:4
- [8]*Jesus answered him, "It is written* (Deuteronomy 6:13)*, 'You shall worship the Lord your God and serve Him only.' "*   Luke 4:8
- [12]*And Jesus answered and said to him, "It is said* (Deuteronomy 6:16)*, 'You shall not put the Lord your God to the test.' "*   Luke 4:12

This is powerful stuff. This is truth that sets people free[19].

God's Word: Counter-Attack

But ... I've made a huge assumption, haven't I? I've made these bold statements about the Word of God at a time when we commonly hear, "The Bible wasn't inspired by God; it was written by men."

I think everyone would agree that the Bible is a book. It's printed and published, bought and sold, read and neglected just like many other books. Although some would say that the Bible is a living book, we know that this can only be true in a figurative sense. There's nothing magical or mystical about the man-made ink, man-made pages, or man-made leather cover of a Bible.

Maybe that's the problem. As far as we can tell, everything about the Bible is man-made ... so it must have come from the minds of men, right?

Not necessarily.

Did you know that Frank Lloyd Wright built more than 530 homes, office buildings, and museums during his lifetime?

It's completely appropriate to say that he 'built' those hundreds of buildings, although he didn't handle the tools and work on any of them himself. Other men constructed the buildings according to Wright's architectural designs.

Regarding the Bible, it's not that it was *either* written by man *or* inspired by God. It's both. About 40 different people, from peasants to kings, from fishermen to lawyers, wrote according to the inspiration of God.

The Bible is the Word of God, in the same way that the buildings are the work of Frank Lloyd Wright.

I've heard people claim that there are contradictions and errors in the Bible, but no one has ever proven that to be true. Claims like this make me wonder: Are we expecting something called *God's Word* to be filled with sheer perfection? Have we found that it isn't? Maybe we'd like to think that a book from God would feature invincible super heroes, like the ones in mythology, rather than imperfect people, like Abraham[20] and Moses[21] and David[22] and Peter[23].

> How was it possible for 40 different writers, spanning 1,600 years, to reveal God's history with people unless there was a single source of inspiration?

The Bible is the intersection of human experience and divine intervention. We read stories of flawed humans and a perfect God. We see sin and consequences. We see redemption and celebration. It only makes sense that God would speak to us from both human and divine perspectives because we're simply ... people, meant to know God.

I think we'd all enjoy knowing God, but our disbelief in the inspiration of his Word hinders us from knowing him the way he wants us to. Let's walk down the path of connection between the Bible and our personal relationship with God and see if this isn't true.

The Holy Spirit inspired the writing of Scripture.

- [16]*All Scripture is inspired by God ...*   *2 Timothy 3:16a*
- [21]*... men moved by the Holy Spirit spoke from God.*   *2 Peter 1:21b*

The inspirer of Scripture lives inside Christians.

- *[16]Do you not know that you are a temple of God and that the Spirit of God dwells in you?*

  1 Corinthians 3:16

The inspirer of Scripture uses Scripture to develop Christians.

- *[16]All Scripture is inspired by God and profitable for teaching, for reproof, for correction, for training in righteousness; [17]so that the man of God may be adequate, equipped for every good work.*

  2 Timothy 3:16-17
- *[10]For we are His workmanship, created in Christ Jesus for good works, which God prepared beforehand so that we would walk in them.* *Ephesians 2:10*

When I deny and knock down the domino called 'The Bible is the inspired Word of God,' it pushes over the domino called, 'The Spirit speaks from Scripture.' This, in turn, falls against the domino called 'Christians are developed to know and serve God.' And once everything has fallen, I stand there, having forsaken my purpose, my hope, and my future in Christ. And somewhere in the shadows is the faint sound of mocking laughter.

Friends, it doesn't have to be this way. It's okay for God to be true[24]. And it's okay for us to live in the truth of his Word.

As I said before, Satan is prowling around, looking for someone to steal from, someone to kill and destroy. If we don't want to become a likely victim, it's important that we know and believe God's Word. We need to stand like Jesus did, or else we'll fall like Eve.

Not only did this chapter begin with the story of Eve's temptation, but we may remember that Chapter 3 began with her story as well. Only that time we gave the account a different ending.

The woman saw that the tree produced good food, that it was beautiful to look at, and that it could make her wise ... **but she told the serpent no.**

The man and his wife heard the sound of the Lord God walking in the garden in the cool of the day, and they ran to be with him.

That outcome, which didn't take place for Eve, is now completely possible for you and me.

The Extra Effort (Search & Rescue)

🖎 *People Sin Against God*—Why does it matter? Taken at face value, what implications does this headline have for the entire human race? ***Important:** Your notes here are will be used in an exercise later in the book.*

_____

_____

_____

🖎 *People Sin Against God*—What difference does it make for you? Think about these statements and summarize your response below.

- I accept the fact that when I feel shame and distance between myself and God that it is a result of my sin.
- I have come clean about the sin in my life and I resist Satan's temptations.

_____

_____

_____

* * *

🖎 If you can, note a recent news story, as well as a personal story, that relates to topics in this chapter.

News: _____

Personal: _____

🙟 List two things that impacted you as you read the chapter or participated in a group discussion.

....

....

....

Scoring for *Search & Rescue* discussion groups:

Read-4 ⸭ *Notes-8* ⸭ *News-1* ⸭ *Personal-2* ⸭ *Impact-16* ⸭ *Total-_____*

1 Information regarding the Book of Jubilees can be found on many credible religious web
  sites, like www.BibleFacts.org.

2 Job 31:33

3 This saying is credited to George Santayana.

4 Revelation 12:9

5 John 10:10

6 1 Peter 5:8

7 Ephesians 6:12

8 2 Corinthians 2:11

9 John 12:31

10 Matthew 4:1-11, Luke 4:1-13

11 John 8:44

12 Romans 5:12

13 Matthew 28:18

14 Revelation 1:18

15 Matthew 22:37-38, Mark 12:29-30

16 Matthew 22:39, Mark 12:31

17 Genesis 2:17

18 Genesis 3:4

19 John 8:31-32

20 Genesis 15:4-6 & Genesis 16:1-6: Abraham tried to self-fulfill God's promise by
  committing adultery.

21 Exodus 3:7 – 4:17: Moses' questions and excuses in response to God's calling caused
  God to be angry with him.

22 2 Samuel 11:2-27: David committed adultery with Bathsheba and set up her husband to
  be killed in battle.

23 Luke 22:54-62: After Jesus had been arrested, Peter denied three times that he even
  knew him.

24 Romans 3:3-4

People Sin Against God

····· The Bad News? | The Good News? | The Good News? ·····

Great Wonders Daily

GOD'S LAW IS GIVEN

*** *Tablets with God's handwriting tossed at crowd of revelers* *** *3000 dead* ***

Mt. Sinai— For the third time in as many days, Israel's leader, Moses, has met directly with God himself. In the two prior meetings, the pair discussed preparations for God's spectacular appearance today. As morning broke, lightning, thunder and trumpet blasts announced God's arrival. Moses brought his people to the base of the mountain where they nervously watched. Moses then spent quite awhile on the mountain as he met with God. He returned some time later with two stone tablets said to contain God's laws in God's handwriting. However, during his absence, a small but unruly crowd had forced Moses' brother to forge a false god. (Ironically, it is reported that God's first Law is, "You must have no other gods before me.") When Moses returned and saw the idol, he hurled the tablets at the unruly crowd. Leaders have now killed about 3000 of the lawbreakers.

Full Story
—*Exodus, chapters 19 through 32*

9 ❧ God's Law Is Given

The Ten Commandments

It's very possible that we bring preconceptions with us as we begin to investigate God's Law. As I write this chapter, Hollywood has marked the 50th Anniversary of Cecil B. DeMille's *The Ten Commandments*, starring Charlton Heston and Yul Brenner. In addition, they've premiered a two-part television mini-series, also called *The Ten Commandments*. I'll have to admit, though, that my mind recalls a different movie image of Moses—"The Lord Jehovah has given unto you these fifteen ... *crash* ... ten commandments for all to obey![1]"

Paul wrote in the New Testament that the Law of Moses "came with glory[2]" when it was given on Mount Sinai. Let's set the scene which leads to Moses' receiving of God's Law by looking at a couple of passages from the Bible. These are God's own words:

> [7]*The Lord said* [to Moses], *"I have surely seen the affliction of My people who are in Egypt, and have given heed to their cry because of their taskmasters, for I am aware of their sufferings.* [8]*So I have come down to deliver them from the power of the Egyptians, and to bring them up from that land to a good and*

spacious land, to a land flowing with milk and honey, to the place of the Canaanite and the Hittite and the Amorite and the Perizzite and the Hivite and the Jebusite. ⁹Now, behold, the cry of the sons of Israel has come to Me; furthermore, I have seen the oppression with which the Egyptians are oppressing them. ¹⁰Therefore, come now, and I will send you to Pharaoh, so that you may bring My people, the sons of Israel, out of Egypt." Exodus 3:7-10

[To the children of Israel, God said,] ⁴'You yourselves have seen what I did to the Egyptians, and how I bore you on eagles' wings, and brought you to Myself. ⁵Now then, if you will indeed obey My voice and keep My covenant, then you shall be My own possession among all the peoples, for all the earth is Mine; ⁶and you shall be to Me a kingdom of priests and a holy nation.' ... Exodus 19:4-6a

Now it may be difficult to *not* picture the fiery finger of God as it burns the following words into the side of the mountain, while a classically-trained Moses buries his face in a robe from the Prop Department, but let's do the best we can.

ONE—*²"I am the Lord your God, who brought you out of the land of Egypt, out of the house of slavery. ³You shall have no other gods before Me.*

TWO—*⁴"You shall not make for yourself an idol, or any likeness of what is in heaven above or on the earth beneath or in the water under the earth. ⁵You shall not worship them or serve them; for I, the Lord your God, am a jealous God, visiting the iniquity of the fathers on the children, on the third and the fourth generations of those who hate Me, ⁶but showing lovingkindness to thousands, to those who love Me and keep My commandments.*

THREE—*⁷"You shall not take the name of the Lord your God in vain, for the Lord will not leave him unpunished who takes His name in vain.*

FOUR—*⁸"Remember the sabbath day, to keep it holy. ⁹Six days you shall labor and do all your work, ¹⁰but the seventh day is a sabbath of the Lord your God; in it you shall not do any work, you or your son or your daughter, your male or your female servant or your cattle or your sojourner who stays with you. ¹¹For in six days the Lord made the heavens and the earth, the sea and all that is in them, and rested on the seventh day; therefore the Lord blessed the sabbath day and made it holy.*

FIVE—*¹²"Honor your father and your mother, that your days may be prolonged in the land which the Lord your God gives you.*

SIX—*¹³"You shall not murder.*

SEVEN—*¹⁴"You shall not commit adultery.*

EIGHT—¹⁵*"You shall not steal.*

NINE—¹⁶*"You shall not bear false witness against your neighbor.*

TEN—¹⁷*"You shall not covet your neighbor's house; you shall not covet your neighbor's wife or his male servant or his female servant or his ox or his donkey or anything that belongs to your neighbor."*

¹⁸*All the people perceived the thunder and the lightning flashes and the sound of the trumpet and the mountain smoking; and when the people saw it, they trembled and stood at a distance.* ¹⁹*Then they said to Moses, "Speak to us yourself and we will listen; but let not God speak to us, or we will die."*

Exodus 20:2-19

* * *

Before we move on, a couple of noteworthy items.

First, there are more than 630 laws which make up God's Law (also referred to as 'the Law' or 'the Law of Moses'). It's only the first set of these laws which we know as the Ten Commandments.

Second, the Catholic Church identifies God's commandments differently than Protestants do. My curiosity about this led me to the following footnote in the *New American Bible* (a very accurate translation), also known as The Catholic Bible.

Traditionally among Catholics verses 1-6 are considered as only one commandment, and verse 17 is considered as two.

God's Primary Purpose for the Law

¹⁹*Now we know that whatever the Law says, it speaks to those who are under the Law, so that every mouth may be closed and all the world may become accountable to God;* ²⁰*because by the works of the Law no flesh will be justified in His sight; for through the Law comes the knowledge of sin.*

Romans 3:19-20

I find this scripture intriguing. It says that there are a couple of results of the Law. The most obvious result is right there at the end of the verse.

• The knowledge of sin comes through the Law.

When my daughter was ten she was learning about the Ten Commandments in a mother-daughter Bible study. She was telling me what she had been learning one day and innocently asked, "How many of the commandments have you broken, Dad?"

"Um … all ten of them … many times."

"Really?"

Then I softly asked her the same question.

I wrote the concept of the first commandment on a piece of paper, and asked, "Has anything in your life been more important to you than God?"

She nodded.

I wrote down the next concept and asked the next question.

By the time we had talked about each of the Ten Commandments, she had voluntarily admitted to breaking seven of them.

Then came a moment which broke my heart.

She pointed at something written in my notes—*pretending you're married to someone else*. She said, "I thought you loved mom."

"I do love mom." I opened a Bible and showed her that Jesus said that *pretending in your mind* is the same as *really pretending with someone*[3]. "I'm sorry, but I have to tell you honestly that I've pretended in my mind."

She looked down at the floor. At that point she didn't want to talk about the Law anymore … and neither did I.

I don't know what those first generations of people were doing with the knowledge of good and evil inside them, but it certainly wasn't what God's Law did with good and evil. The Law spelled out sin in black and white, loud and clear. And now that our human race knows exactly what sin is, the other result of the Law, mentioned in Romans 3:19, comes to light.

- The Law speaks so that every mouth may be closed and all the world may become accountable to God.

> God's Law isn't the personal growth and spiritual development program we all hoped it would be.

Take another look at that phrase "every mouth may be closed." Do you think it could be another way of saying that all of our excuses have been taken away? This entire statement draws a vivid picture of a courtroom in my mind. Because of the Law, we stand accountable before the Eternal Judge of heaven. Our rationalizing has failed. All talking is done. Now, we stand silently as our guilt is revealed, and our sentence is determined.

Look at the Ten Commandments as they appear elsewhere in the Bible. Do you see the real consequence of breaking God's Law?

ONE—14"You shall not follow other gods, any of the gods of the peoples who surround you, 15for the Lord your God in the midst of you is a jealous God; otherwise the anger of the Lord your God will be kindled against you, and He will wipe you off the face of the earth."   *Deuteronomy 6:14-15*

TWO—25"When you become the father of children and children's children and have remained long in the land, and act corruptly, and make an idol in the form of anything, and do that which is evil in the sight of the Lord your God so as to provoke Him to anger, 26I call heaven and earth to witness against you today, that you will surely perish quickly from the land where you are going over the Jordan to possess it. You shall not live long on it, but will be utterly destroyed."   *Deuteronomy 4:25-26*

THREE—16'Moreover, the one who blasphemes the name of the Lord shall surely be put to death; all the congregation shall certainly stone him. The alien as well as the native, when he blasphemes the Name, shall be put to death.'   *Leviticus 24:16*

FOUR—14'Therefore you are to observe the sabbath, for it is holy to you. Everyone who profanes it shall surely be put to death; for whoever does any work on it, that person shall be cut off from among his people. 15For six days work may be done, but on the seventh day there is a sabbath of complete rest, holy to the Lord; whoever does any work on the sabbath day shall surely be put to death.'   *Exodus 31:14-15*

FIVE—9'If there is anyone who curses his father or his mother, he shall surely be put to death; he has cursed his father or his mother, his bloodguiltiness is upon him.'   *Leviticus 20:9*

SIX—17'If a man takes the life of any human being, he shall surely be put to death.'   *Leviticus 24:17*

SEVEN—10'If there is a man who commits adultery with another man's wife, one who commits adultery with his friend's wife, the adulterer and the adulteress shall surely be put to death.'   *Leviticus 20:10*

EIGHT—2"If the thief is caught while breaking in and is struck so that he dies, there will be no bloodguiltiness on his account."   *Exodus 22:2*

[In essence, he got what he deserved.]

NINE & TEN—… 29being filled with all unrighteousness, wickedness, greed, evil; **#10—full of envy**, murder, strife, **#9—deceit**, malice; they are gossips, 30slanderers, haters of God, insolent, arrogant, boastful, inventors of evil, disobedient to parents, 31without understanding, untrustworthy, unloving, unmerciful; 32and although they know the ordinance of God, that **those who practice such things are worthy of death**, they not only do the same, but also give hearty approval to those who practice them. *Romans 1:29-32 [emphasis added]*

Each of the Ten Commandments carries a death penalty. James, the half-brother of Jesus, wrote that if we stumble in regard to one of the commandments, we've become guilty concerning them all[4].

And what we won't find hidden somewhere in God's Law is a little card that reads: *Thanks for trying. Try again tomorrow.*

God didn't give us the Law so that we could try again. He gave it so that we would know that we're separated from him and that, because of our sins, a death penalty hangs over our heads. Moses saw this effect from the Law immediately. Even before the tablets had a chance to cool down, three thousand sinners had already been killed (see Exodus 32 for the details).

I believe that the Law is the reason there's such an overwhelming sense of condemnation and judgment throughout the Old Testament. From the time of Moses and Joshua, through the time of the Judges, the Kings, and the Prophets of Israel, the Law did what it was meant to do. It pronounced a death penalty against everyone who sinned.

But then Jesus Christ stepped into the picture and something seemed different. Conversations about God's Law took on new dimensions.

Jesus, Pharisees, and Me

> [Jesus said,] [17]*"Do not think that I came to abolish the Law or the Prophets; I did not come to abolish but to fulfill.* [18]*For truly I say to you, until heaven and earth pass away, not the smallest letter or stroke shall pass from the Law until all is accomplished."*
>
> *Matthew 5:17-18*

When Jesus said that he would *fulfill the Law*, that *the Law would be accomplished*, it's possible that he was saying that he intended to *live a perfect life*, never breaking any of God's commandments. It makes sense, after all, because Jesus did just that. You may remember our conversation from Chapter 4 about his blood and how, being the only begotten son of God, he lived a sinless life. Although it's possible that *fulfill the Law* meant *live a perfect life*, it's really not likely.

There were other people who, just like Jesus, didn't want to "abolish the Law or the Prophets." They were called Pharisees, the most prominent group of religious leaders of Jesus' time. Their primary focus in life was to 'live perfectly by the Law.'

If by *fulfill* and *accomplished*, Jesus meant *living up to the standard of the Law*, then he and the Pharisees would have been in complete agreement. They would have been one another's biggest supporters.

But they weren't. The Pharisees were the greatest source of opposition to Jesus' message. In a scathing indictment against them, Jesus called the Pharisees hypocrites, blind guides, fools, and serpents[5].

Many Christians today believe that God's Law is a moral standard to be lived up to. They focus on it like it's the ultimate set of boundaries, the best guide for a happy life. That's not at all how Jesus viewed the Law. But that's exactly what the Pharisees believed it to be.

The Pharisees were by no means the best example of spiritually healthy people. There's a principle that says "good thinking creates good behavior, which creates good results. In the same manner, bad thinking creates bad behavior, which creates bad results[6]." The Pharisees *thought* something to be true about God's Law that wasn't. They *behaved* in a way that benefited no one. And the *result* was that they plotted against their own Messiah.

We can't afford to believe the way the Pharisees did, or else we'll see in our lives the type of behavior they demonstrated. And the result will be that we won't see Jesus for who he is but will treat him in a way that he doesn't deserve.

When I talk about the Pharisees like this, I'm talking about something called *legalism*. Although legalism is often described simply as 'living by do's and don'ts,' it's actually more than this. Real legalism is living by a list of rules and regulations *in order to capture God's love or to avoid his anger*. That's a very important phrase, although many people seem to be unaware of it. Legalism has nothing to do with having a 'standard for moral behavior,' but instead describes the 'unhealthy motivation' behind someone's morality.

The Do's and The Don'ts

It's true. Some people live with an unhealthy motivation behind their Christianity. I was at a men's Bible study at a local restaurant. The group leader said, "When the Law convicts us of our sin, it has done exactly what it was meant to do." Although several of us nodded in agreement, one of the men shot out of his seat, halfway over the breakfast table, almost shouting, "But don't take the Law away from me! If I don't have it, there's nothing to keep me from sinning."

I've written and rewritten this section a number of times, focused on the nuts and bolts of doctrine. This time I'm praying that God will help me speak the truth from a caring human heart. I'd really like to help that man, and others like him, down from the table.

People hope to gain God's acceptance. They hope to avoid his anger. Someone told them on a Sunday morning that following this or that checklist will result in the outcome they desire. Someone said that if the good in a person's life outweighs the bad, then on Judgment Day heaven will be theirs. So, on the way to Sunday dinner, an unconscious decision was made; either to live by *The Do's* or to live by *The Don'ts*.

The Do's: Living in hope that God will accept me. What I'm calling *The Do's* can be described as the belief that good behavior on our part will cause God to love us, bless us, or treat us as special. Now this *sounds* wonderful, although psychologists might ask how 'conditional love' could be healthy between God and people when it's unhealthy in human relationships.

Honestly, I don't think anyone ever embraces *The Do's* by thinking it through like this. But because 'thinking determines behavior and behavior produces specific results,' we can get an idea of what people are thinking because we can see their behavior and its results.

The behavior of people who live by *The Do's* tends to look something like this. 'Doers' displays Christian artwork and scripture plaques in their home. They are cause-oriented, big on traditions and national pride. They fold their hands when praying in public restaurants.

[There's nothing wrong with any of the good behaviors I've mentioned so far. Remember, legalism has to do with an 'unhealthy motivation' behind a person's morality. And I haven't identified anything suggesting a Doer's motivation yet.]

Legalism is not 'good behavior,' but rather 'unhealthy motivation' behind good behavior.

Doers carry a Bible with them wherever they go. They pray long, beautiful prayers out loud and quote scripture from a specific Bible translation. They gather with like-minded people and keep members of other kinds of churches at arms-length. They resist things they don't understand, like divine healing and miracles. They wince at the mention of 'worldly' issues.

[More than likely, we're beginning to see question marks at this point, but we still haven't identified the 'Doer'-kind of legalism.]

Doers say, "I may not be perfect, but at least I don't fill-in-the-blank like that guy." They seem competitive around other Doers. They question the lifestyles of other Christians, holding them up to their own convictions. They jokingly "mock" other church denominations and split hairs regarding Bible teaching. They accuse, blame, and judge others.

Now, there's some strong evidence of unhealthy motivation.

Ladies and gentlemen ... a legalist.

This type of person is *not* a legalist because of any good behavior he or she may be engaged in. They are *not* legalists because they gather with like-minded people, resist things they don't understand, or wince at worldliness—

although they might find additional guidance helpful. This person is a legalist because they consider themselves righteous and view others with contempt.

> 9*And [Jesus] also told this parable to some people who trusted in themselves that they were righteous, and viewed others with contempt:* 10*"Two men went up into the temple to pray, one a Pharisee and the other a tax collector.* 11*The Pharisee stood and was praying this to himself: 'God, I thank You that I am not like other people: swindlers, unjust, adulterers, or even like this tax collector.* 12*I fast twice a week; I pay tithes of all that I get.'* 13*But the tax collector, standing some distance away, was even unwilling to lift up his eyes to heaven, but was beating his breast, saying, 'God, be merciful to me, the sinner!'* 14*I tell you, this man went to his house justified rather than the other; for everyone who exalts himself will be humbled, but he who humbles himself will be exalted."* Luke 18:9-14

Jesus taught our lesson much better than I did. Did you see it?

God's Law set standards for religious activity, like going into the temple, praying, fasting, and tithing. But engaging in these good practices wasn't the reason Jesus condemned the Pharisee. Jesus made an example of him because the Pharisee *thought* that he was righteous and viewed others with contempt. He *behaved* selfishly and the *result* was that he was not justified by God.

There's a way out of this kind of legalism and it's revealed by looking at the way in to it—*someone told them to follow the list and that if the good in their life outweighs the bad, then heaven will be theirs.* Or in other words, we can do things to deserve God's goodness. The word for this is *religion.*

> [Jesus said,] 22*"Many will say to Me on that day, 'Lord, Lord, did we not prophesy in Your name, and in Your name cast out demons, and in Your name perform many miracles?'* [—all good things] 23*And then I will declare to them, 'I never knew you; depart from Me, you who practice lawlessness.'"* Matthew 7:22-23

"I never knew you?" The word for Jesus knowing you is *relationship.*

Here's the bottom line regarding *The Do's.* Good behavior based on religion counts for nothing. Good behavior resulting from our friendship with God is actually what counts.

But then there's also something called *The Don'ts.*

The Don'ts: Living in hope that I will avoid God's anger. Just days before I wrote these very words, I prayed with a man who confessed a life of heartache and sin. With tears and remorse he told me that he would continue to ask for prayer until things changed. But each time I offered encouragement from the Bible, he would respond, "I'm wicked. There's evil inside me." Although this man hadn't actually 'lived his life' by *The Don'ts*, the effects of *The Don'ts* had certainly shown up.

If you smoke, drink, cuss, or act up in any way, God's going to get you!

This is how a sermon on *The Don'ts* can be summarized. And there are all kinds of supporting verses in the Bible that talk about 'acting up,' as well as 'God getting you.' These verses are generally found in the Old Testament, primarily in the Law. In my opinion, a sermon on *The Don'ts* is easy to preach when there are no real issues to be dealt with.

But life happens. And when it happens in an ugly way, the Christian who has been listening to teaching regarding *The Don'ts* draws an unhealthy conclusion.

I lost my job—or worse—*because God is punishing me.*

This is a message found in one of the oldest books of the Bible, the Book of Job. Job was a man who had lost everything; his children, his wealth, and finally his health. Three of Job's friends came to sympathize and comfort him in his pain. The problem was, in trying to explain that God caused bad things to happen in Job's life to teach him a lesson, they were absolutely wrong. God himself told one of the men, "I'm angry with you and your two friends, because you have not spoken about me correctly[7]."

Here are just a few of the statements they made about God.

[8]... those who plow iniquity and those who sow trouble harvest it. [9]By the breath of God they perish, and by the blast of His anger they come to an end.   Job 4:8b-9

[17]... do not despise the discipline of the Almighty. [18]For He inflicts pain, and gives relief; He wounds, and His hands also heal.   Job 5:17b-18

[4]If your sons sinned against Him, then He delivered them into the power of their transgression.   Job 8:4

Here's something that's key. Let's not miss this. One of Job's friends said that sinners "come to an end by the blast of his anger." Next thing you know, God is saying to this very man, "I'm angry with you." So what do you think he was expecting next?

From the end of the story we know that what this man and the other two friends actually received from God ... was an opportunity to experience his forgiveness. Keep this truth in mind. We're coming back to it.

I want you to know that 'Job's three friends' are still hanging around today. I know a woman who lost a baby during childbirth due to a cancerous tumor that had gone undetected. Within one day of returning home, Christians arrived on her doorstep with warm casserole dishes and the 'comforting' message that this had happened to her because of her sin. Thankfully, she wasn't living by *The Don'ts* and she rejected their message.

I think that's all I care to say about those who spread the message of *The Don'ts*. I'm sure you can guess where we might end up if I continue.

The person I've wanted to talk about instead—actually, *talk with*—is the one who has picked up this message and found it too heavy to carry. While *The Do's* tend to produce self-righteous and judgmental people, *The Don'ts* commonly result in people who are paralyzed by guilt and shame. And sadly, this describes what seems to be a great number of Christians.

Earlier, we read Jesus' parable about the Pharisee who viewed others with contempt. A tax collector was also mentioned in the parable. And many of us can identify with him. Like the tax collector, we've acknowledged that fact that we're sinners.

The man I recently prayed with kept saying, "I'm wicked. There's evil inside me." This tends to be our response to a perfect moral standard. It also tends to be our response to a perfectly holy God. But where we go next with our guilt and shame is the key to everything. Will we go back to the Law and try harder? Why? "According to the Law … without shedding of blood there is no forgiveness[8]." Or will we go to God himself and, like the tax collector, cry out to receive his mercy?

My heart breaks because many people find it impossible to believe that God could actually love and forgive them. They feel that God is angry and disgusted by them. The tax collector prayed from a distance, refusing to look up toward heaven; some feel so distant from heaven that they refuse to pray.

I want to point us all in the direction of mercy, because mercy is the only way out of this kind of legalism. And mercy is revealed when we understand what Jesus really meant when he said that he would *fulfill the Law*.

"I Have Come to Fulfill the Law."

We've seen that Paul made a couple of points regarding God's purpose behind the Law.

- The knowledge of sin comes through the Law.

- The Law speaks so that every mouth may be closed and all the world may become accountable to God.

We're asking what it meant for Jesus to fulfill the Law. One question which could lead us to a proper understanding would be this: Did Jesus ever say or do anything that supported Paul's two points?

[Jesus said,] *²¹"You have heard that the ancients were told, 'You shall not commit murder' and 'Whoever commits murder shall be liable to the court.' ²²But I say to you that everyone who is angry with his brother shall be guilty before the court; and whoever says to his brother, 'You good-for-nothing,' shall be guilty before the supreme court; and whoever says, 'You fool,' shall be guilty enough to go into the fiery hell."* Matthew 5:21-22

the teaching continues ...

²⁷"You have heard that it was said, 'You shall not commit adultery'; ²⁸but I say to you that everyone who looks at a woman with lust for her has already committed adultery with her in his heart." Matthew 5:27-28

The knowledge of sin comes through the law. When I read these words from Jesus, "You have heard that it was said," I see a crowd of non-murderers and non-adulterers responding, "Amen, brother!" But when Jesus reveals that sin is a disease of the heart more than a problem of behavior, every non-lawbreaker lowers his or her head in shame as well. Everyone realizes that when it comes to lawbreakers, there's no such thing as 'us' and 'them.' Each of us is condemned.

This was one of the major themes in the teachings of Jesus, but sometimes we don't learn from what we're taught. Sometimes it takes a humiliating experience for us to understand a lesson.

³The scribes and the Pharisees brought a woman caught in adultery, and having set her in the center of the court, ⁴they said to Him, "Teacher, this woman has been caught in adultery, in the very act. ⁵Now in the Law Moses commanded us to stone such women; what then do You say?" ⁶They were saying this, testing Him, so that they might have grounds for accusing Him. But Jesus stooped down and with His finger wrote on the ground. ⁷But when they persisted in asking Him, He straightened up, and said to them, "He who is without sin among you, let him be the first to throw a stone at her." ⁸Again He stooped down and wrote on the ground. ⁹When they heard it, they began to go out one by one, beginning with the older ones, and He was left alone, and the woman, where she was, in the center of the court. ¹⁰Straightening up, Jesus said to her, "Woman, where are they? Did no one condemn you?" ¹¹She said, "No one, Lord." And Jesus said, "I do not condemn you, either. Go. From now on sin no more."

John 8:3-11

The Law speaks so that every mouth may be closed and all the world may become accountable to God.

How humiliating! I'm not just talking about the woman. I'm talking about the scribes and Pharisees, too. How must it have felt for these supporters and defenders of God's Law to have their own consciences betray them publicly?

It's been suggested that Jesus writing on the ground is an important aspect of the story. Maybe he wrote specific sins that had been committed by the woman's accusers. Or maybe, for the second time in human history, the finger of God was imprinting the Ten Commandments on the earth. The Bible doesn't say what he wrote.

But we do know this. Both the woman and her accusers were silenced and convicted. If there were bystanders watching this story play out, I'm sure that the same thing happened to them. As a matter of fact, I'm feeling it myself just reading the story 2,000 years later.

Every mouth *is* closed. The world *is* accountable to God. And under the Law, there's only one result that we can expect: execution.

So how could Jesus offer the woman mercy ... unless he knew that someone other than her would be executed in her place?

⁶³... And the high priest said to him, "I adjure You by the living God, that You tell us whether You are the Christ, the Son of God." ⁶⁴Jesus said to him, "You have said it yourself; nevertheless I tell you, hereafter you will see the Son of Man sitting at the right hand of Power, and coming on the clouds of heaven."

⁶⁵Then the high priest tore his robes and said, "He has blasphemed! What further need do we have of witnesses? Behold, you have now heard the blasphemy; ⁶⁶what do you think?" They answered, "He deserves death!"

Matthew 26:63b-66

¹³... having forgiven us all our transgressions, ¹⁴having canceled out the certificate of debt consisting of decrees against us [the Law], which was hostile to us; and He has taken it out of the way, having nailed it to the cross.

Colossians 2:13b-14

In every way, Jesus Christ fulfilled the Law.

The Extra Effort (Search & Rescue)

❧ *God's Law Is Given*—Why does it matter? Taken at face value, what implications does this headline have for the entire human race? ***Important: Your notes here will be used in an exercise later in the book.***

❧ *God's Law Is Given*—What difference does it make for you? Think about these statements and summarize your response below.

- I do not try to close the distance I feel from God by living up to a list of do's and don'ts.
- I know how the crucifixion of Jesus was God's antidote for the effects of the Law.

* * *

❧ If you can, note a recent news story, as well as a personal story, that relates to topics in this chapter.

News:

Personal:

Part III: Follow the Path

ॐ List two things that impacted you as you read the chapter or participated in a group discussion.

_____

_____

_____

Scoring for *Search & Rescue* discussion groups:

Read-4 * *Notes-8* * *News-1* * *Personal-2* * *Impact-16* * *Total-_____*

[1] This line comes from the hit comedy movie *History of the World: Part I.*

[2] 2 Corinthians 3:7

[3] Matthew 5:27-28

[4] James 2:10

[5] Matthew 23—the entire chapter

[6] Joe Calhoon & Bruce Jeffrey, <u>Prioritize! A System for Leading Your Business and Life on Purpose</u> (Sevierville, TN: Insight Publishing, 2005), 23.

[7] Job 42:7-8

[8] Hebrews 9:22

Great Wonders Daily

JESUS CHRIST DIES

*** *Night descends at noon as self-proclaimed Messiah executed* *** Romans claims, *"This man was the Son of God."* ***

Jerusalem— Never has a Roman execution attracted so much attention. Jesus of Nazareth, a self-styled jewish teacher, was crucified under Roman authority today. However, Governor Pilate rejected responsibility for the punishment. Jewish leaders arrested their criminal late last night and released him into

Roman hands early this morning. The man was accused of claiming he was God, a highly unusual accusation to deserve death. A Roman soldier present at the execution said that he thought the man to be the Son of God, but few local citizens in the crowd that gathered throughout the afternoon shared the opinion.

Roman authorities had begun weighing their options for crowd control when the afternoon sky began to turn as black as night, sending the crowd back to their homes. Sources indicate that this also seemed to be about the time that Jesus succumbed to death.

Full Story

—*Luke Chapter 23*

10 ❧ Jesus Christ *Dies*

[1]♀: "What's inside the box?"

♂: "A gift."

♀: "Who's it for?"

♂: "It's for you."

♀: "Well, what is it?"

♂: "Would you believe that what's actually in the box ...

... is *exactly* what's in the box?"

♀: "If I said yes, would you be any closer to giving it to me?"

♂: "And what you may believe to be inside the box ...

... may not be what's inside the box."

♀: "Stop. You're teasing me."

♂: "Happy anniversary. I love you."

* * *

Good Friday Behind Glass

I need to set this first story up a bit. When I was writing the original edition of this book, someone told me that he could see the *8 Great Wonders* as a set of teaching videos. I smiled politely as I thought about the number of zeros in the total cost for a project like that. The next time I met with my ministry partner Sam, he told me to "be praying about that video idea. I sense that there's something to it." So I began praying half-hearted prayers. Then, trusted friends began saying things like "Your book is very visual," and "I can actually see you doing this stuff on video."

All right, God, I get it!

The next thing I knew I was being introduced to a video producer named Joe, and we began the process of filming a ministry promotional video.

As Joe began to develop ideas, he called me over to his home to meet Gorman, a filmmaker from California. And it's here that the story begins.

"Eric, share with Gorman and me your vision for presenting the crucifixion of Jesus on video."

I smiled.

God wants each of us to be affected by the event of Jesus' death. This is certainly true. But I want to steer people away from the idea that the crucifixion isn't real until we somehow 'believe it' to be real. Whatever happened the day Jesus died for us, happened. It's an event from history, frozen in time. Our belief doesn't make it more real. Our doubt doesn't take anything away from it. So I'm going to put the crucifixion behind glass.

When I was a boy my family visited a natural history museum, and I saw several life-sized dioramas depicting events from the past. I remember the impression that our visit left on me. So my idea is to invite people to join us, via the video, on a tour through the *Great Wonders Museum*. Let's show them four specific moments from Christ's Passion, as described by the writers of the Gospels. And let's tell them what was happening behind the scenes, from the perspective of those who wrote the New Testament letters.

Scene #1: All the Faces in the Crowd

> [26]*When they led Him away, they seized a man, Simon of Cyrene, coming in from the country, and placed on him the cross to carry behind Jesus.*

27And following Him was a large crowd of the people, and of women who were mourning and lamenting Him. 28But Jesus turning to them said, "Daughters of Jerusalem, stop weeping for Me, but weep for yourselves and for your children. 29For behold, the days are coming when they will say, 'Blessed are the barren, and the wombs that never bore, and the breasts that never nursed.' 30Then they will begin to say to the mountains, 'Fall on us,' and to the hills, 'Cover us.' 31For if they do these things when the tree is green, what will happen when it is dry?"

32Two others also, who were criminals, were being led away to be put to death with Him.

Luke 23:26-32

22Then they brought Him to the place Golgotha, which is translated, Place of a Skull.

Mark 15:22

☙ What details do you think we would see behind the glass in a display of *Scene #1: All the Faces in the Crowd*?

....

....

There's a tour guide who will say something like "A few of you have noticed the song playing softly in the background; *Via Dolorosa*. A number of the most beautiful Christian songs we've ever heard were written to remember the events of the crucifixion of Jesus."

"Yes, sir. I'm sure we'll be hearing *The Old Rugged Cross* in just a few minutes."

Whatever the lead-in may be, we'll definitely hear the tour guide explain that Jesus Christ died for the ungodly, he died for us all, for everyone[2].

6For while we were still helpless, at the right time Christ died for the ungodly.

Romans 5:6

8But God demonstrates His own love toward us, in that while we were yet sinners, Christ died for us.

Romans 5:8

9But we do see Him who was made for a little while lower than the angels, namely, Jesus, because of the suffering of death crowned with glory and honor, so that by the grace of God He might taste death for everyone.

Hebrews 2:9

The visitors will hear that Jesus died because of our transgressions, another name for our sins[3].

25He who was delivered over because of our transgressions, ...   *Romans 4:25a*

21He made Him who knew no sin to be sin on our behalf, so that we might become the righteousness of God in Him.   *2 Corinthians 5:21*

And sure, it's a big Bible word, but let's go ahead and have the guide explain what *propitiation* means; that Jesus died in our place, that he was our substitute[4].

... 2and He Himself is the propitiation for our sins; and not for ours only, but also for those of the whole world.   *1 John 2:2*

The guide will then have the visitors follow him to the next diorama, the next scene. Maybe the viewers at home will notice; maybe they won't, but mine will be one of the faces in the crowd.

Scene #2: From Separated to Reconciled

23They tried to give Him wine mixed with myrrh; but He did not take it.

Mark 15:23

34But Jesus was saying, "Father, forgive them; for they do not know what they are doing."   *Luke 23:34a*

23Then the soldiers, when they had crucified Jesus, took His outer garments and made four parts, a part to every soldier and also the tunic; now the tunic was seamless, woven in one piece. 24So they said to one another, "Let us not tear it, but cast lots for it, to decide whose it shall be"; this was to fulfill the Scripture: "They divided My outer garments among them, and for My clothing they cast lots." 25Therefore the soldiers did these things. ...   *John 19:23-25a*

27They crucified two robbers with Him, one on His right and one on His left. 28And the Scripture was fulfilled which says, "And He was numbered with transgressors." 29Those passing by were hurling abuse at Him, wagging their heads, and saying, "Ha! You who are going to destroy the temple and rebuild it in three days, 30save Yourself, and come down from the cross!" 31In the same way the chief priests also, along with the scribes, were mocking Him among themselves and saying, "He saved others; He cannot save Himself. ³²Let this Christ, the King of Israel, now come down from the cross, so that we may see and believe!" Those who were crucified with Him were also insulting Him.

Mark 15:27-32

¹⁹Pilate also wrote an inscription and put it on the cross. It was written, "JESUS THE NAZARENE, THE KING OF THE JEWS." ²⁰Therefore many of the Jews read this inscription, for the place where Jesus was crucified was near the city; and it was written in Hebrew, Latin and in Greek. ²¹So the chief priests of the Jews were saying to Pilate, "Do not write, 'The King of the Jews'; but that He said, 'I am King of the Jews.' " ²²Pilate answered, "What I have written I have written."

John 19:19-22

³⁹One of the criminals who were hanged there was hurling abuse at Him, saying, "Are You not the Christ? Save Yourself and us!" ⁴⁰But the other answered, and rebuking him said, "Do you not even fear God, since you are under the same sentence of condemnation? ⁴¹And we indeed are suffering justly, for we are receiving what we deserve for our deeds; but this man has done nothing wrong." ⁴²And he was saying, "Jesus, remember me when You come in Your kingdom!" ⁴³And He said to him, "Truly I say to you, today you shall be with Me in Paradise."

Luke 23:39-43

²⁵... But standing by the cross of Jesus were His mother, and His mother's sister, Mary the wife of Clopas, and Mary Magdalene. ²⁶When Jesus then saw His mother, and the disciple whom He loved standing nearby, He said to His mother, "Woman, behold, your son!" ²⁷Then He said to the disciple, "Behold, your mother!" From that hour the disciple took her into his own household.

John 19:25b-27

∽ What details do you think we would see behind the glass in a display of *Scene #2: From Separated to Reconciled?*

As the visitors are looking at the details of the second scene, the guide will say, "Through the sacrifice of Jesus for our sins, the separation experienced in the Garden of Eden has been reversed. All of God's enemies—people—are now reconciled to him5."

10For if while we were enemies we were reconciled to God through the death of His Son, much more, having been reconciled, we shall be saved by His life.

Romans 5:10

Now it's real subtle, but something catches my attention and I'm almost sure that I saw something move behind the glass. My eyes dart back and forth, looking for what may have just moved.

It must have been my imagination.

Then, something else catches my eye. Although his face is somewhat turned away, that soldier hanging Pilate's inscription above Jesus ... no, it can't be ... he looks a little like me.

We're asked to move to the third diorama. I keep looking back.

Scene #3: What Exactly is Finished?

45Now from the sixth hour darkness fell upon all the land until the ninth hour. 46About the ninth hour Jesus cried out with a loud voice, saying, "Eli, Eli, lama sabachthani?" that is, "My God, My God, why have You forsaken Me?" 47And some of those who were standing there, when they heard it, began saying, "This man is calling for Elijah."

Matthew 27:45-47

28After this, Jesus, knowing that all things had already been accomplished, to fulfill the Scripture, said, "I am thirsty."

John 19:28

48Immediately one of them ran, and taking a sponge, he filled it with sour wine and put it on a reed, and gave Him a drink. 49But the rest of them said, "Let us see whether Elijah will come to save Him."

Matthew 27:48-49

30Therefore when Jesus had received the sour wine, He said, "It is finished!"

John 19:30a

46And Jesus, crying out with a loud voice, said, "Father, into Your hands I commit My spirit." Having said this, He breathed His last.

Luke 23:46

51And behold, the veil of the temple was torn in two from top to bottom; and the earth shook and the rocks were split. 52The tombs were opened, and many

*bodies of the saints who had fallen asleep were raised; ... ⁵⁴Now the centurion,
and those who were with him keeping guard over Jesus, when they saw the
earthquake and the things that were happening, became very frightened and
said, "Truly this was the Son of God!"*   Matthew 27:51-52, 54

*⁴⁸And all the crowds who came together for this spectacle, when they observed
what had happened, began to return, beating their breasts.*   Luke 23:48

*⁴⁰There were also some women looking on from a distance, among whom
were Mary Magdalene, and Mary the mother of James the Less and Joses, and
Salome. ⁴¹When He was in Galilee, they used to follow Him and minister to Him;
and there were many other women who came up with Him to Jerusalem.*
                                                           Mark 15:40-41

☙ What details do you think we would see behind the glass in a display of *Scene
#3: What Exactly is Finished?*

I'm fidgeting with my wrists, rubbing them as the guide says, "The Law
against us is cancelled[6]."

*... ¹⁴having canceled out the certificate of debt consisting of decrees against us,
which was hostile to us; and He has taken it out of the way, having nailed it to
the cross.*   Colossians 2:14

The guide will say, "Because of Jesus Christ's death for us, we are
justified." He explains that he learned in Sunday school that *justified* means *'just
as if I'd'* never sinned.
    "We are redeemed, or bought back, and we are forgiven[7]."

*⁹Much more then, having now been justified by His blood, we shall be saved
from the wrath of God through Him.*   Romans 5:9

*... ⁵so that He might redeem those who were under the Law, that we might
receive the adoption as sons.*   Galatians 4:5

7In Him we have redemption through His blood, the forgiveness of our trespasses, according to the riches of His grace ...

Ephesians 1:7

Suddenly, I can't move my legs. My entire body is in pain. "What's happening to me?" I see the lips of the guide moving, but I can't hear him.

I turn to look at Jesus, but I can't see any further than my own reflection in the glass. When I try to look at the cross, I can't see beyond myself.

"Please, sir, this way," the guide says.

Scene #4: Dead, For Sure

31Then the Jews, because it was the day of preparation, so that the bodies would not remain on the cross on the Sabbath (for that Sabbath was a high day), asked Pilate that their legs might be broken, and that they might be taken away. 32So the soldiers came, and broke the legs of the first man and of the other who was crucified with Him; 33but coming to Jesus, when they saw that He was already dead, they did not break His legs. 34But one of the soldiers pierced His side with a spear, and immediately blood and water came out. 35And he who has seen has testified, and his testimony is true; and he knows that he is telling the truth, so that you also may believe. 36For these things came to pass to fulfill the Scripture, "Not a bone of Him shall be broken." 37And again another Scripture says, "They shall look on Him whom they pierced."

John 19:31-37

☙ What details do you think we would see behind the glass in a display of *Scene #4: Dead, For Sure?*

I grab my side and scream as the spear is driven into Jesus' side.

Now, instead of me looking through the glass at the scene, the scene is looking at me. And I'm being buried in the sand of a huge hour glass.

The guide says, "Everything we've seen at the cross is true for each and every human being. It's true for you; it's true for me. There is, however, one obstacle yet to overcome." He taps on the hour glass.

"When Jesus Christ died for us, we died with him[8]."

14For the love of Christ controls us, having concluded this, that one died for all, therefore all died; ...

2 Corinthians 5:14

11It is a trustworthy statement: For if we died with Him, we will also live with Him; ...

2 Timothy 2:11

The guide is looking at a Bible in his hand when he says, "Because of this, we all must be born again."

6For the gospel has for this purpose been preached even to those who are dead, that though they are judged in the flesh as men, they may live in the spirit according to the will of God.

1 Peter 4:6

I eased back into Joe's leather desk chair. I could see that something creative was going on behind Gorman's eyes, but he wasn't ready to tip his hand. He looked at Joe and said, "We couldn't do this scene justice for less than a hundred grand."

I knew it.

What's Inside the Box?

Here's some brutally honest truth. Despite the fact that Jesus Christ died for our sins, Christians still commit sin. Despite the fact that we were reconciled to God through the death of his son, we still feel distant from him *when* we sin. And despite the fact that God has forgiven us completely, we still feel guilt and shame *because* of our sin. As if we weren't really reconciled and forgiven; as if the crucifixion of Jesus didn't really work. Then we fall into a degenerative process which, in technical terms, is called *trying harder to behave better.* And when we blow it yet again, we find that trying harder doesn't work.

My wife and I once visited a church, and at the end of the service they had a unique time of personal prayer. Not what I had seen in the past, where people come to the edge of the platform up front and are prayed for by the pastor or others; rather, we were told to find someone sitting nearby who needed God's encouragement. My wife turned to the friends we were sitting with, so I moved in another direction. Standing at the opposite end of our row, about 10 to 12 empty chairs away from me, were two young women. And one of them was crying.

I walked over and asked if I could pray with her. She nodded. I asked her to tell me what was happening.

"Every time I feel good about moving forward in my relationship with God, Satan comes to my mind and harasses me about my past."

A thought came to me. "What if Satan accused you of being an astronaut?"

She looked at me as if I was crazy. I've seen this look often enough to know what it is.

"Would you believe him?"

She was silent.

"Maybe you *are* an astronaut. I mean, you've probably been through the astronaut training program, haven't you?"

"No." (Thank goodness she started to play along.)

"Well, at least you've spent time down at Cape Canaveral in south Florida?"

"No."

"You've toured Mission Control in Houston?"

She shook her head.

"Do you know what the initials in NASA stand for?"

"I'm not sure."

"So, if Satan accused you of being an astronaut you wouldn't believe him … because you're really something else, aren't you?"

She half-smiled.

"Doesn't the Bible say that when you became a Christian you became a new person, that old things went away, and that new things have come9?"

Her head lifted and she stood a bit taller.

I encouraged her, "The next time you're accused of being a dirty, rotten scoundrel, tell Satan that's who you used to be, but somebody new is living inside you now."

She nodded. And then you should have heard the amazing prayer she prayed. *Show me, strengthen me, remind me.*

I haven't seen her since, but I have to believe that things began to change for her for the better. Not because of a silly astronaut analogy, but because she was reminded that salvation *is* what it is—the new birth of our spirit in the image of God. Likewise, if we're ever going to see guilt become less powerful in our lives, we have to see that the crucifixion of Jesus is what it is—the very moment in history when God drew near to us, the moment he was no longer holding anything against us. Reconciliation and forgiveness are written in stone. God really was in Christ, reconciling the world to himself. He really isn't counting our sins against us10. Belief doesn't make it more real, and doubt can't remove what's in God's heart.

"But, Eric, my sin … you don't know what I've done."

What matters more is that we know what God did through Jesus on the cross. Since we have no control over the love that God has for us, the only right thing to do is to receive the gift inside the sealed box—receive the relationship and mercy that came through Jesus' death on the cross. It's in our best interest to stop fighting Jesus on these issues. Let's surrender to his love. Let's confess our sin, come clean, and thank God for the reality of his nearness and forgiveness. Then, let's get on with it and move forward in our relationship with him.

It *is* finished!

May we all experience the blessing of what's really real.

The Extra Effort (Search & Rescue)

Jesus Christ Dies—Why does it matter? Taken at face value, what implications does this headline have for the entire human race? **Important:** *Your notes here will be used in an exercise later in the book.*

Jesus Christ Dies—What difference does it make for you? Think about these statements and summarize your response below.
- I understand that when Jesus died, everyone died with him.
- I believe that reconciliation and forgiveness came into God's heart completely the day Jesus died.

----

* * *

☙ If you can, note a recent news story, as well as a personal story, that relates to topics in this chapter.

News:

Personal:

☙ List two things that impacted you as you read the chapter or participated in a group discussion.

Scoring for *Search & Rescue* discussion groups:

Read-4 ∗ Notes-8 ∗ News-1 ∗ Personal-2 ∗ Impact-16 ∗ Total-_____

---

[1] ♀ is the symbol for male and ♂ is the symbol for female.

[2] Jesus Christ died for the ungodly, he died for us all, for everyone. See also 1
Thessalonians 5:10, 1 John 3:16, Romans 8:32, and 1 Timothy 2:6.

[3] Jesus died because of our transgressions, another name for our sins. See also Romans
6:10, 1 Corinthians 15:3, Hebrews 1:3, Hebrews 10:12, and 1 John 3:5.

[4] *Propitiation* means that Jesus died in our place, that he was our substitute. See also
Romans 3:25, Hebrews 2:17, and 1 John 4:10.

[5] Through the sacrifice of Jesus for our sins, the separation experienced in the Garden of
Eden has been reversed. All of God's enemies—people—are now reconciled to him. See
also Colossians 1:20-22, 1 Peter 3:18, and Ephesians 2:13.

[6] The Law against us is cancelled. See also Romans 8:3-4.

[7] Because of Jesus Christ's death for us, we are justified. *Justified* means 'just as if I'd'
never sinned. We are redeemed, or bought back, and we are forgiven. See also Romans
3:24, Hebrews 9:12, Hebrews 9:15, Colossians 1:14, and Colossians 2:13.

[8] Everything we've seen at the cross is true for each and every human being. It's true for
you; it's true for me. There is, however, one obstacle yet to overcome. When Jesus Christ
died for us, we died with him. See also Romans 6:5-6, Romans 7:4, Galatians 2:20,
Galatians 6:14, Colossians 2:20, and 1 Peter 2:24.

[9] 2 Corinthians 5:17

[10] 2 Corinthians 5:19

Great Wonders Daily

JESUS, ALIVE AGAIN!

*** Confirmed: Tomb is empty! *** Disciples claim resurrection, guards claim body was stolen ***

Jerusalem— Very early this morning, controversy erupted when the tomb containing the dead body of Jesus of Nazareth was found empty. Several Jewish women, friends of the deceased, arrived at the empty tomb to carry out Jewish burial customs. They said they found Roman guards asleep at the site, a crime punishable by death. The guards could not be reached for comment. How the body was removed remains a mystery. The guards had been placed at the tomb because Jewish leaders worried something like this was going to happen. Sources say Jesus told people openly before he died that he would be raised from the dead. Rumors already abound that this is exactly what took place in the wee hours of the morning.

Full Story

—Matthew, chapter 28
Mark, chapter 16
John, chapter 20

A Legend's New Sound | Rescued Miners: Hungry, Dehydrated But Safe

11 ❧ Jesus, Alive Again!

The Moment Everything Changed

I've talked about the prayer I prayed the day my dad was rushed to the emergency room, the day my beliefs were crushed. *Something has gone wrong, God, and it has everything to do with what I believe. Show me how everything fits together. Show me the truth.* I haven't really mentioned the details of *how* the Holy Spirit answered that prayer ... until now.

I want to take you back to an exact moment in my life. I still have a vivid picture of it in my mind. It took place only a matter of weeks after my prayer in front of the hospital.

I was picking up my wife from work, pulling up to the entrance way to her building's parking lot. I was scanning the AM stations on my car radio.

A Bible teacher was answering a caller's question, and he was talking about something he referred to as *the neglected half of the gospel*. He had my full attention immediately.

As I sat in my car, waiting for my wife to come down from her office, the teacher explained that the reason Jesus Christ had come was to "give spiritually dead people *life*." To that point, I hadn't heard the gospel message in those terms.

In his book, *Classic Christianity*[1], Bob George, the Bible teacher I was listening to, tells the story of an experience of his that mirrors my first exposure to the message of *life* that day. In the middle of a difficult time, wondering what he could have missed, Bob heard God speak to him about a specific scripture from the Bible.

> [10]*For if while we were enemies we were reconciled to God through the death of His Son, much more, having been reconciled, we shall be saved by His life.*
>
> *Romans 5:10*

God began to answer my desperate prayer with this scripture also. That was the moment he began to show me the truth.

I began sharing this verse with others, and found myself quoting it this way: "While we were enemies, past tense, we were reconciled to God, past tense, through the death of His Son. Having been reconciled, past tense, we shall be saved, *future tense*, by His life."

Through this scripture, God showed me that we are reconciled enemies who need *life* ... in order to become friends of God.

As I learned more and more that our primary need is to receive *life*, it seemed that someone had rewritten my Bible, putting the word everywhere.

> [21]*For if a law had been given which was able to impart life, then righteousness would indeed have been based on law.*   *Galatians 3:21*

A man named John was one of the first people Jesus called to follow him. He was with Jesus throughout his entire ministry, even standing at the foot of the cross as Jesus was crucified. In his writings, John referred to himself as "the disciple that Jesus loved," something that's true for each Christian.

When I read the teachings of Jesus recorded by John, the '*life* meter' went absolutely nuts.

> [21]*"For just as the Father raises the dead and gives them life, even so the Son also gives life to whom He wishes. ...*
>
> [24]*Truly, truly, I say to you, he who hears My word, and believes Him who sent Me, has eternal life, and does not come into judgment, but has passed out of death into life.* [25]*Truly, truly, I say to you, an hour is coming and now is, when the dead will hear the voice of the Son of God, and those who hear will live.* [26]*For just as the Father has life in Himself, even so He gave to the Son also to have life in Himself; ..."*
>
> *John 5:21, 24-26*

⁹"I am the door; if anyone enters through Me, he will be saved, and will go in and out and find pasture. ¹⁰The thief comes only to steal and kill and destroy; I came that they may have life, and have it abundantly."   John 10:9-10

⁶Jesus said to him, "I am the way, and the truth, and the life; no one comes to the Father but through Me."   John 14:6

John understood that *life* was the central message of salvation, and he taught it to others. He also said that it was the motivation behind his writings.

¹⁴We know that we have passed out of death into life, because we love the brethren. He who does not love abides in death.   1 John 3:14

¹¹And the testimony is this, that God has given us eternal life, and this life is in His Son. ¹²He who has the Son has the life; he who does not have the Son of God does not have the life. ¹³These things I have written to you who believe in the name of the Son of God, so that you may know that you have eternal life.   1 John 5:11-13

³¹but these have been written so that you may believe that Jesus is the Christ, the Son of God; and that believing you may have life in His name.   John 20:31

We've seen that Paul was *convinced* that we died with Christ and *compelled* to reach people with the Gospel. Here's a glimpse of John's motivation for reaching people with the Gospel.

¹⁸They laid hands on the apostles [John being one of them] *and put them in a public jail. ¹⁹But during the night an angel of the Lord opened the gates of the prison, and taking them out he said, ²⁰"Go, stand and speak to the people in the temple the whole message of this Life."*   Acts 5:18-20

At this point, I had to test my 'rewritten Bible' theory. "All right, God, let's see if you put *life* in the Old Testament."

¹⁹"I call heaven and earth to witness against you today, that I have set before you life and death, the blessing and the curse. So choose life in order that you may live, you and your descendants, ²⁰by loving the Lord your God, by obeying His voice, and by holding fast to Him; for this is your life and the length of your days, that you may live in the land which the Lord swore to your fathers, to Abraham, Isaac, and Jacob, to give them."

Deuteronomy 30:19-20

[14]*"I will put My Spirit within you and you will come to life, and I will place you on your own land. Then you will know that I, the Lord, have spoken and done it, declares the Lord."*

Ezekiel 37:14

"Okay, God, at this point you're just showing off."

The Resurrection: Unbelievable, Yet ...

Someone once told me that 3 in 10 people disagree with the Bible, in regard to the teaching that Jesus Christ was physically resurrected from the dead. I don't know if the numbers are correct, but to a certain degree I understand the opinion. After all, the bottom line of Bible teaching is that one person out of the eight billion[2] or so who have ever lived on this planet was raised from the dead and is still alive today—2,000 years later. It sounds like a complete fairy tale.

No one actually saw the resurrection of Jesus take place. There were no video cameras, no audio recorders inside the tomb. No one was sitting there to see what happened the exact moment he was raised to life.

In the last chapter we focused heavily on the circumstances surrounding the event of the crucifixion. But when it comes to the resurrection, the emphasis isn't on the *event* so much as it is on the *person* who was raised.

A number of people experienced the resurrected Jesus face-to-face. You might be a little surprised to learn that it was a significant number of people.

The Resurrection of Jesus

[1]*When the Sabbath was over, Mary Magdalene, and Mary the mother of James, and Salome, bought spices, so that they might come and anoint Him.* [2]*Very early on the first day of the week, they came to the tomb when the sun had risen.* [3]*They were saying to one another, "Who will roll away the stone for us from the entrance of the tomb?"*

Mark 16:1-3

[2]*And behold, a severe earthquake had occurred, for an angel of the Lord descended from heaven and came and rolled away the stone and sat upon it.* [3]*And his appearance was like lightning, and his clothing as white as snow.* [4]*The guards shook for fear of him and became like dead men.* [5]*The angel said to the women, "Do not be afraid; for I know that you are looking for Jesus who has*

been crucified. ⁶He is not here, for He has risen, just as He said. Come, see the
place where He was lying."
Matthew 28:2-6

⁵Entering the tomb, they saw a young man sitting at the right, wearing a white
robe; and they were amazed.
Mark 16:5

... ⁵and as the women were terrified and bowed their faces to the ground, the
men said to them, "Why do you seek the living One among the dead? ⁶He is not
here, but He has risen. Remember how He spoke to you while He was still in
Galilee, ⁷saying that the Son of Man must be delivered into the hands of sinful
men, and be crucified, and the third day rise again." ⁸And they remembered His
words, ...
Luke 24:5-8

⁷"But go, tell His disciples and Peter, 'He is going ahead of you to Galilee; there
you will see Him, just as He told you.'"
Mark 16:7

⁸And they left the tomb quickly with fear and great joy and ran to report it
to His disciples.
Matthew 28:8

Interestingly, the first to experience the Resurrected Jesus may have been the guards. One moment they were keeping each other awake with tales of personal glory and crude jokes. The next, the ground was quaking and an angel was rolling away the stone. Needless to say, they dropped like flies. Even after accepting bribes to change their story, they knew what really happened.

Peter and John See the Empty Tomb

... ⁹and [the women] returned from the tomb and reported all these things to the
eleven and to all the rest. ¹⁰Now they were Mary Magdalene and Joanna and
Mary the mother of James; also the other women with them were telling these
things to the apostles.
Luke 24:9-10

²So [Mary Magdalene] ran and came to Simon Peter and to the other disciple
whom Jesus loved, and said to them, "They have taken away the Lord out of the
tomb, and we do not know where they have laid Him." ³So Peter and the other
disciple went forth, and they were going to the tomb. ⁴The two were running
together; and the other disciple ran ahead faster than Peter and came to the
tomb first; ⁵and stooping and looking in, he saw the linen wrappings lying
there; but he did not go in. ⁶And so Simon Peter also came, following him, and

entered the tomb; and he saw the linen wrappings lying there, ⁷and the face-cloth which had been on His head, not lying with the linen wrappings, but rolled up in a place by itself. ⁸So the other disciple who had first come to the tomb then also entered, and he saw and believed. ⁹For as yet they did not understand the Scripture, that He must rise again from the dead. ¹⁰So the disciples went away again to their own homes.

John 20:2-10

Jesus Appears to Mary Magdalene

¹¹But Mary was standing outside the tomb weeping; and so, as she wept, she stooped and looked into the tomb; ¹²and she saw two angels in white sitting, one at the head and one at the feet, where the body of Jesus had been lying. ¹³And they said to her, "Woman, why are you weeping?" She said to them, "Because they have taken away my Lord, and I do not know where they have laid Him." ¹⁴When she had said this, she turned around and saw Jesus standing there, and did not know that it was Jesus. ¹⁵Jesus said to her, "Woman, why are you weeping? Whom are you seeking?" Supposing Him to be the gardener, she said to Him, "Sir, if you have carried Him away, tell me where you have laid Him, and I will take Him away." ¹⁶Jesus said to her, "Mary!" She turned and said to Him in Hebrew, "Rabboni!" (which means, Teacher). ¹⁷Jesus said to her, "Stop clinging to Me, for I have not yet ascended to the Father; but go to My brethren and say to them, 'I ascend to My Father and your Father, and My God and your God.' "

John 20:11-17

¹⁰She went and reported to those who had been with Him, while they were mourning and weeping. ¹¹When they heard that He was alive and had been seen by her, they refused to believe it.

Mark 16:10-11

Jesus Appears to the Women

⁹And behold, Jesus met [the women] and greeted them. And they came up and took hold of His feet and worshiped Him. ¹⁰Then Jesus said to them, "Do not be afraid; go and take word to My brethren to leave for Galilee, and there they will see Me."

Matthew 28:9-10

After Mary Magdalene and the other women saw Jesus, he appeared to two men on their way to a town called Emmaus. Then Jesus appeared to Peter, then to all the Apostles, and then to over 500 of his disciples at one time. He spent a total of 40 days with his followers. And for all these people, the excitement wasn't based on the fact that a tomb somewhere was empty. It was based on the truth that the Lord who loved them was with them.

Ten days after Jesus ascended into heaven the Holy Spirit came and empowered these people to preach publicly that Jesus was raised, that Jesus is Lord. It had only been less than two months since Jesus had been crucified, and the very first time his disciples proclaimed resurrection—this fairy tale, if you will—3,000 devout Jews actually believed them and were baptized.

Those disciples who had actually heard, seen, and touched Jesus after his resurrection never changed their story. What they told governors and kings while they were bound in chains is also what they wrote to persecuted churches to encourage them to endure. We know that the 11 Apostles never wavered from the resurrection story even though it ultimately resulted in a brutal death for at least 10 of them.

We've come a long way from *10 of 11 of them* being martyred due to their belief in the physical resurrection of Jesus, to *3 in 10 of us* denying that it ever took place that way.

... Impossible to *Live* Without

12Now if Christ is preached, that He has been raised from the dead, how do some among you say that there is no resurrection of the dead? 13But if there is no resurrection of the dead, not even Christ has been raised; 14and if Christ has not been raised, then our preaching is vain, your faith also is vain. 15Moreover we are even found to be false witnesses of God, because we testified against God that He raised Christ, whom He did not raise, if in fact the dead are not raised. 16For if the dead are not raised, not even Christ has been raised; 17and if Christ has not been raised, your faith is worthless; you are still in your sins. 18Then those also who have fallen asleep in Christ have perished. 19If we have hoped in Christ in this life only, we are of all men most to be pitied.

20But now Christ has been raised from the dead, the first fruits of those who are asleep. 21For since by a man came death, by a man also came the resurrection of the dead. 22For as in Adam all die, so also in Christ all will be made alive. 23But each in his own order: Christ the first fruits, after that those who are Christ's at His coming, ...   1 Corinthians 15:12-23

Unlike any other belief system, Christianity teaches that belief only matters if our leader is living today, more than 2,000 years after his birth. Paul tells us plainly in this passage that our beliefs are in vain if the resurrection of Jesus Christ didn't take place. He doesn't even allow us to consider that a religion based on a dead leader can be possible. (What if we substituted *The Buddha, Confucius, Socrates, Plato, Aristotle, Muhammad*, or any other name in the place of the name *Christ* in the verses 14 and 17 of the passage we just read?)

Religious leaders throughout the ages have taught different paths to God. Many have developed followers, and several have established world religions. Many have even died for their beliefs. But Jesus' resurrection separates him from every other religious leader who has ever lived. As impacting as his teachings are, as selfless as Jesus' death on the cross was, as large as his influence has been, the real power of Christian faith in God rests 100% upon the reality of Christ's resurrection. No other religious leader is qualified to give us life, saving us from spiritual death. Simply put, if Jesus didn't rise from the dead, there's absolutely no hope at all.

Behind-the-Scenes

I want us to study three groups of New Testament verses which give us a behind-the-scenes look at the resurrection. <u>Underline</u> or highlight phrases which, in your opinion, communicate an important truth. Note your observations.

#1: The Risen Lord

- ⁶*Remember Jesus Christ, risen from the dead, descendant of David, according to my gospel, ...*
  2 Timothy 2:8

- ⁴*... that He was raised on the third day according to the Scriptures, ...*
  1 Corinthians 15:4b

- *... ⁴who was declared the Son of God with power by the resurrection from the dead, according to the Spirit of holiness, Jesus Christ our Lord, ...*
  Romans 1:4

- *... ⁹knowing that Christ, having been raised from the dead, is never to die again; death no longer is master over Him.*
  Romans 6:9

- ¹⁸*He is also head of the body, the church; and He is the beginning, the firstborn from the dead, so that He Himself will come to have first place in everything.*
  Colossians 1:18

- ⁹*For to this end Christ died and lived again, that He might be Lord both of the dead and of the living.*
  Romans 14:9

- *... ¹⁹and [know] what is the surpassing greatness of His power toward us who believe. These are in accordance with the working of the strength of His might ²⁰which He brought about in Christ, when He raised Him from the dead and seated Him at His right hand in the heavenly places, ...*
  Ephesians 1:19-20

☙ How would you summarize these scriptures regarding *The Risen Lord*? What do you feel was the most important truth you read?

_____

_____

_____

Not only does the resurrection say something about who Jesus is, but it also says something about God's intentions for each of us.

#2: The Offer of Salvation

- *¹⁹For as through the one man's disobedience the many were made sinners, even so through the obedience of the One the many will be made righteous.*

    Romans 5:19

- *⁵For if we have become united with Him in the likeness of His death, certainly we shall also be in the likeness of His resurrection, ...*   *Romans 6:5*

- *¹⁰For if while we were enemies we were reconciled to God through the death of His Son, much more, having been reconciled, we shall be saved by His life.*   *Romans 5:10*

- *¹⁴Now God has not only raised the Lord, but will also raise us up through His power.*   *1 Corinthians 6:14*

- *⁴For indeed He was crucified because of weakness, yet He lives because of the power of God. For we also are weak in Him, yet we will live with Him because of the power of God directed toward you.*   *2 Corinthians 13:4*

- *⁹... if you confess with your mouth Jesus as Lord, and believe in your heart that God raised Him from the dead, you will be saved; ...*   *Romans 10:9*

- *... ¹⁴knowing that He who raised the Lord Jesus will raise us also with Jesus and will present us with you.*   *2 Corinthians 4:14*

☙ How would you summarize these scriptures regarding *The Offer of Salvation*? What do you feel was the most important truth you read?

_____

_____

_____

- *³Blessed be the God and Father of our Lord Jesus Christ, who according to His great mercy has caused us to be born again to a living hope through the resurrection of Jesus Christ from the dead, ...* *1 Peter 1:3*

- *... ¹²having been buried with Him in baptism, in which you were also raised up with Him through faith in the working of God, who raised Him from the dead. ¹³When you were dead in your transgressions and the uncircumcision of your flesh, He made you alive together with Him, having forgiven us all our transgressions, ¹⁴having canceled out the certificate of debt consisting of decrees against us, which was hostile to us; and He has taken it out of the way, having nailed it to the cross.* *Colossians 2:12-14*

- *¹¹But if the Spirit of Him who raised Jesus from the dead dwells in you, He who raised Christ Jesus from the dead will also give life to your mortal bodies through His Spirit who dwells in you.* *Romans 8:11*

- *⁴Therefore we have been buried with Him through baptism into death, so that as Christ was raised from the dead through the glory of the Father, so we too might walk in newness of life.* *Romans 6:4*

- *... ¹⁰that I may know Him and the power of His resurrection ...* *Philippians 3:10a*

- *... ⁴so that you might be joined to another, to Him who was raised from the dead, in order that we might bear fruit for God.* *Romans 7:4b*

- *⁴But God, being rich in mercy, because of His great love with which He loved us, ⁵even when we were dead in our transgressions, made us alive together with Christ (by grace you have been saved), ⁶and raised us up with Him, and seated us with Him in the heavenly places in Christ Jesus, ⁷so that in the ages to come He might show the surpassing riches of His grace in kindness toward us in Christ Jesus.* *Ephesians 2:4-7*

- *¹Therefore if you have been raised up with Christ, keep seeking the things above, where Christ is, seated at the right hand of God.* *Colossians 3:1*

- *... ¹⁰and to wait for His Son from heaven, whom He raised from the dead, that is Jesus, who rescues us from the wrath to come.* *1 Thessalonians 1:10*

☙ How would you summarize these scriptures regarding *The Life That Follows*? What do you feel was the most important truth you read?

....

....

....

....

A Thing Called Hope

Paul wrote that faith, hope and love will last forever, and that the greatest of these is love[3].

I see patterns everywhere. And this thought is no exception. As I see it, the story of Christ, both from the Bible and from our lives personally, is a story that begins with hope, unfolds with faith, and results in love. I believe that we need faith in order to experience God's love personally, but we must have hope before we can know what faith is.

Many people came to Jesus for solutions to their problems when he ministered on this earth. They came to him with doubts; "Lord, I believe. Help my unbelief[4]." They came to him with hesitancy; "If you want to ... you can make me clean[5]." But I believe that everyone was prompted by hope. Hope got them out of their houses and put them on the road to Jesus.

I remember discussing with a friend why the woman with hemorrhage problems thought that touching the edge of Jesus' clothing could heal her[6]. He pointed out an Old Testament scripture that reads, "The sun of righteousness will rise with healing in his wings[7]." He told me that word for *wings* in Hebrew, the original language of the Old Testament, also describes the tassels on the hem of a Jewish prayer shawl; like the kind Jesus would have worn. The woman knew what the scriptures said. She saw what Jesus was doing. And I'm sure a thought like this came to her: *If anybody can, he can.* Now that's hope.

Seedlings of hope sprang up all around the ministry of Jesus, but hope fully came into existence the morning Jesus rose from the dead. If anybody can save us, if anybody can bring us back from the dead and lead us to where God means us to be, Jesus Christ can. His resurrection was proof that "with God anything is possible[8]."

Now, here's where it hits home for each of us. What's the name of the person you know, who people have described as a lost cause? Who's too far gone because of drugs or alcohol? Who's too perverted and evil to ever become a Christian? If we know Christ and the power of his resurrection, then we know there's hope for this person after all. And if so, what keeps us from praying for them?

People can talk about the Hope Diamond, the Cape of Good Hope, and even Bob Hope; if we want to really know it, if we want hope to pick us up out of ourselves and lead us to where Jesus is, we have to see his resurrection for what it truly is—the moment of greatest and unrivaled hope, the moment relationship with God became possible.

We interrupt this Bible study for a special bulletin ...

--- The Bad News? | *Great Wonder's Daily* | The Good News? *---*

*SPECIAL EDITION * SPECIAL EDITION * SPECIAL EDITION * SPECIAL EDITION *

ANOTHER WONDER WONDER IDENTIFIED?

*** *Supporters propose "9 Wonders" initiative* *** *Debate begins* ***

Jerusalem — Could it be that there are nine fine wonders in human history? In an upper conference room, it was announced today that the headline *God's Holy Spirit Is Given* should be identified as the sixth of nine wonders in God's history with people. Supporters of the nine wonders theory suggested that "the outpouring of the Holy Spirit, 50 days after Christ's resurrection, qualifies as a wonder, being an event from history which can impact the lives of every human being." The new headline was compared to *God's Law Is Given*. Experts pointed out that "only the indwelling Holy Spirit can accomplish what people had hoped God's Law would do in their lives." They summed up their presentation by stating that "the outpouring of God's Spirit bridges the gap between Christ's rising from the dead and any individual's acceptance of the free gift of salvation." The author of *The 8 Great Wonders of Human History* offered no comment but was seen scratching his head.

Part III: Follow the Path

I'm sure you remember my story about the man who shot out of his seat, halfway over the breakfast table, shouting, "But don't take the Law away from me! If I don't have it, there's nothing to keep me from sinning."

When I heard the man's comment, my first thought was, *What about the Holy Spirit?*

After all, if we've committed ourselves to developing a relationship with God, looking for the leading of his Spirit and listening for his voice, would we ever have to be concerned about moral boundaries? Would the Holy Spirit ever lead us to commit sin?

"But, Eric, many people don't live the kind of life you're talking about."

So God offers us an optional Plan B? *I want you to be led by my Spirit, but if, for some reason, that's no good for you, then you can live by my Law instead.*

I'm reacting foolishly, of course.

The real issue has nothing to do with people weighing the pros and cons of 'living by the Law' and 'living by the Holy Spirit' and concluding that religion is better than relationship. The real issue is that, statistically, only a third of the people who are considered to be 'born again' actually believe that the Holy Spirit is real[9]. And since two-thirds of born again people wouldn't be looking to a 'nonexistent' Holy Spirit to establish morality in their lives, then, by default, the prevailing standard would have to be 'living by the Ten Commandments.'

ॐ There are eight comparisons in the following passage of scripture. <u>Underline</u> them in the passage *and* write them down on the following page. The first one has already been done.

[2]You are our letter, written in our hearts, known and read by all men; [3]being manifested that you are a letter of Christ, cared for by us, <u>written not with ink but with the Spirit of the living God</u>, not on tablets of stone but on tablets of human hearts. [4]Such confidence we have through Christ toward God. [5]Not that we are adequate in ourselves to consider anything as coming from ourselves, but our adequacy is from God, [6]who also made us adequate as servants of a new covenant, not of the letter but of the Spirit; for the letter kills, but the Spirit gives life. [7]But if the ministry of death, in letters engraved on stones, came with glory, so that the sons of Israel could not look intently at the face of Moses because of the glory of his face, fading as it was, [8]how will the ministry of the Spirit fail to be even more with glory? [9]For if the ministry of condemnation has glory, much

more does the ministry of righteousness abound in glory. ¹⁰For indeed what had

glory, in this case has no glory because of the glory that surpasses it. ¹¹For if

that which fades away was with glory, much more that which remains is in

glory. ¹²Therefore having such a hope, we use great boldness in our speech,

2 Corinthians 3:2-12

written not with ink	but with the Spirit of the living God
not on	but on
not that	but our
not of the	but of the
for the	but the
ministry of	ministry of
ministry of	ministry of
that which	that which

The column on the left describes God's Law; the column on the right, God's Holy Spirit.

I'm sure we remember the *Separated, Condemned, Executed* chapter, where we saw that spiritual death is a process. Isn't it interesting that in the verses we just studied, Paul called the Law "the ministry of death" and "the ministry of condemnation"? And he said that there are new ministries in effect these days.

The prominent words we find contrasted to the Law are *Spirit, life,* and *righteousness.* But there's one more word that needs to be added to our list, and it's found several times in each of the following scriptures.

¹³For the promise to Abraham or to his descendants that he would be heir of the

world was not through the Law, but through the righteousness of faith. ¹⁴For if

those who are of the Law are heirs, faith is made void and the promise is

nullified; ¹⁵for the Law brings about wrath, but where there is no law, there also

is no violation. ¹⁶For this reason it is by faith, in order that it may be in accordance with grace, so that the promise will be guaranteed to all the descendants, not only to those who are of the Law, but also to those who are of the faith of Abraham, who is the father of us all,   Romans 4:13-16

[16]nevertheless knowing that a man is not justified by the works of the Law but through faith in Christ Jesus, even we have believed in Christ Jesus, so that we may be justified by faith in Christ and not by the works of the Law; since by the works of the Law no flesh will be justified.   Galatians 2:16

[2]This is the only thing I want to find out from you: did you receive the Spirit by the works of the Law, or by hearing with faith? [3]Are you so foolish? Having begun by the Spirit, are you now being perfected by the flesh? [4]Did you suffer so many things in vain—if indeed it was in vain? [5]So then, does He who provides you with the Spirit and works miracles among you, do it by the works of the Law, or by hearing with faith?   Galatians 3:2-5

[22]But the Scripture has shut up everyone under sin, so that the promise by faith in Jesus Christ might be given to those who believe. [23]But before faith came, we were kept in custody under the law, being shut up to the faith which was later to be revealed. [24]Therefore the Law has become our tutor to lead us to Christ, so that we may be justified by faith. [25]But now that faith has come, we are no longer under a tutor.   Galatians 3:22-25

Paul traveled thousands of miles, preaching the message of faith in Jesus Christ in cities where no one had ever heard it before. The people Paul ministered to were Gentiles. These non-Jewish people had no idea what living by the Law of Moses meant. But as they began to embrace of message of a relationship with God through Jesus, Paul made an interesting observation.

[14]For when Gentiles who do not have the Law do instinctively the things of the Law, these, not having the Law, are a law to themselves, [15]in that they show the work of the Law written in their hearts, their conscience bearing witness and their thoughts alternately accusing or else defending them, ...   Romans 2:14-15

How can we "do instinctively the things of the Law, not having the Law"?
Spirit.
Life.
Righteousness.
And faith.

¹Therefore there is now no condemnation for those who are in Christ Jesus. ²For the law of the Spirit of life in Christ Jesus has set you free from the law of sin and of death. ³For what the Law could not do, weak as it was through the flesh, God did: sending His own Son in the likeness of sinful flesh and as an offering for sin, He condemned sin in the flesh, ⁴so that the requirement of the Law might be fulfilled in us, who do not walk according to the flesh but according to the Spirit.

Romans 8:1-4

¹⁸But if you are led by the Spirit, you are not under the Law.

Galatians 5:18

Here's one last comparison of the Law and the Spirit that I'd like for us to see. First, a New Testament assessment of the Old Testament Law:

¹⁴... their minds were hardened; for until this very day at the reading of the old covenant the same veil remains unlifted, ... ¹⁵But to this day whenever Moses is read, a veil lies over their heart; ...

2 Corinthians 3:14a & 15

And regarding the Holy Spirit; here's an Old Testament promise of a New Testament truth.

²⁶"Moreover, I will give you a new heart and put a new spirit within you; and I will remove the heart of stone from your flesh and give you a heart of flesh. ²⁷I will put My Spirit within you and cause you to walk in My statutes, and you will be careful to observe My ordinances."

Ezekiel 36:26-27

Somehow, all of us need to experience the fulfillment of Ezekiel's prophecy in our lives.

Part III: Follow the Path

The Extra Effort (Search & Rescue)

☙ *Jesus, Alive Again!*—Why does it matter? Taken at face value, what implications does this headline have for the entire human race? ***Important: Your notes here will be used in an exercise later in the book.***

☙ *Jesus, Alive Again!*—What difference does it make for you? Think about these statements and summarize your response below.
- I know the incredible hope that exists for us because Jesus was raised from the dead, as well as the dire hopelessness if he wasn't.
- I understand how Jesus is the only way to God.

* * *

☙ If you can, note a recent news story, as well as a personal story, that relates to topics in this chapter.

News:

Personal:

❧ List two things that impacted you as you read the chapter or participated in a group discussion.

Scoring for *Search & Rescue* discussion groups:

*Read-4 * Notes-8 * News-1 * Personal-2 * Impact-16 * Total-_____*

[1] Bob George, <u>Classic Christianity: Life's Too Short to Miss the Real Thing</u> (Eugene: Harvest House, 1989), p. 45.

[2] Laverna Patterson (Biochemistry, B.S. 1982) states on her web site that "in my calculation, the total population during the flood may have been 15 to 33 million. The total population since Creation is about eight billion." She is the only individual I have found who suggests a total number of human beings who have existed.

[3] 1 Corinthians 13:13

[4] Mark 9:24

[5] Matthew 8:2

[6] Matthew 9:20-22, Mark 5:25-34, Luke 8:43-48

[7] Malachi 4:2

[8] Matthew 19:26, Mark 10:27, Luke 18:27

[9] This statement is based on raw data from *The Barna Group*—86% of 313 evangelical/born again individuals, and 22% of 1,316 non-evangelical/born again individuals believe that the Holy Spirit actually exists.

Great Wonders Daily

your name ACCEPTS SALVATION

*** "I once was lost, but now am found!" *** Choice has joyous results ***

editorial— I once pulled a trivia game card that asked, "What is the name of the song played at the end of every Billy Graham service?" I guessed the only religious tune I knew, Amazing Grace. Funny thing about the question and my answer; I was familiar with both, but understood neither. I'd seen Billy Graham on TV. I'd seen people pour from the stands at his call to receive Jesus Christ as their personal Savior. But I never paid attention to the song being sung in the background. Each time I watched, I said to myself, "What are those people thinking," or singing, in regard to Amazing Grace. I wasn't even sure it was a religious song. I'd often heard it sung in a pub. Much has changed since then. Now I know that *Just As I Am* is the song they sing after a Billy Graham message. I know what people are thinking when they respond to accept Christ into their heart and life, and I know what's so amazing about grace because I've experienced it for myself. Have you?

Related Story
—Acts 2

12 ❧ <u>your name</u> Accepts Salvation

I loaned my grandfather a copy of Billy Graham's autobiography and asked him to read it.

The two men were from the same generation and had similar rural backgrounds. I thought maybe there would be a connection there. Actually, I was hoping to use the book as a bridge to a conversation about my relationship with Jesus Christ. Granddad was a very intelligent man. And since he was family, I had always been a little intimidated to mention matters of faith to him.

A speed reader, he finished the book in just a matter of days.

During our visit afterwards, Granddad told me that he didn't think we could believe the Bible for what it says. And he used the story of *Jonah and the Whale* as an example. He told me that a whale's throat is too small to swallow a human being. Therefore, the story must be an allegory; not fact. Of course, I *wanted* to tell him that according to Jonah 1:17, it wasn't a whale that swallowed the prophet; that "the Lord appointed a great *fish* to swallow Jonah, and Jonah was in the stomach of the *fish* three days and three nights." But the truth may have been even harder for him to believe. Besides, he wasn't feeling well that night and excused himself just a short time later.

It was the last conversation the two of us ever had.

* * *

The First Ones to Accept Salvation

One hundred twenty men and women were filled with the Holy Spirit when he was sent to empower Christians on the day of Pentecost. They all began speaking the mighty deeds of God[1]. Then, Peter preached a sermon which couldn't have lasted ten minutes, and 3,000 people believed his message and were baptized[2]. It's likely that only weeks had passed when the number of people who believed came to be about 5,000. Even at that point, 'believers in the Lord' were constantly added[3] and the Word of God kept on spreading[4].

Although thousands accepted salvation in a very short amount of time, the Bible does record how a few individuals came to be the first Christians. We can read the incredible testimonies of Simon—who was involved in the occult[5], an Ethiopian eunuch—who was a royal official in the Queen's court[6], Saul—a persecutor of Christians[7], Cornelius—a Roman centurion who also gathered his relatives and close friends to hear the message[8], Sergius Paulus—an intelligent man who was associated with a false prophet and occult practitioner[9], Lydia—a reverent businesswoman[10], a jailer in Philippi—who was about to commit suicide[11], and Crispus—a synagogue leader[12]. Each of these individuals responded to the message of the gospel.

> ... *13for "Whoever will call on the name of the Lord will be saved."*
>
> *14How then will they call on Him in whom they have not believed? How will they believe in Him whom they have not heard? And how will they hear without a preacher? 15How will they preach unless they are sent? Just as it is written, "How beautiful are the feet of those who bring good news of good things!"*
>
> Romans 10:13-15

> *15And [Jesus] said to them, "Go into all the world and preach the gospel to all creation. 16He who has believed and has been baptized shall be saved; but he who has disbelieved shall be condemned."*
>
> Mark 16:15-16

> *18For the word of the cross is foolishness to those who are perishing, but to us who are being saved it is the power of God. ... 21For since in the wisdom of God the world through its wisdom did not come to know God, God was well-pleased through the foolishness of the message preached to save those who believe.*
>
> 1 Corinthians 1:18, 21

¹⁵So, for my part, I am eager to preach the gospel to you also who are in Rome.

¹⁶For I am not ashamed of the gospel, for it is the power of God for salvation to everyone who believes, to the Jew first and also to the Greek.   Romans 1:15-16

⁸... "The word is near you, in your mouth and in your heart"—that is, the word of faith which we are preaching, ⁹that if you confess with your mouth Jesus as Lord, and believe in your heart that God raised Him from the dead, you will be saved; ...   Romans 10:8b-9

Clueless Ministries

I graduated high school with absolutely no idea of what I wanted to do with the rest of my life. Being a 'creative-type,' I tried my hand at songwriting and album cover design, but nothing panned out. I found myself in broken-hearted prayer one night, with tears rolling down my cheeks. "God, what do *you* want me to do?" The answer came fairly quickly and I knew that he was calling me to share the gospel with people. He was calling me to be an evangelist.

If I would have chosen a name for a ministry back then, the only name that would have fit was *Clueless Ministries*. My best guess of what it meant for me to be an evangelist was to stand on the corner of Elm and East Main with a bullhorn in my hand, shouting "Jesus loves you" to everybody in my hometown. Thankfully, God intervened before any of that could happen. Although I had been called, I wasn't prepared.

About a year earlier I had written a movie script in which the main character encounters a Christian. This excerpt shows exactly where I was at personally in my understanding of the gospel message.

> **CHRISTIAN.** When God sees a Christian, He sees that Jesus Christ is in that person's heart. That individual came to see his need for Jesus because no one had a way to pay for their sins until Jesus died on the cross. Anyone who does not accept Jesus' payment will be sentenced to eternal death because the wages of sin is death, but the gift of God is eternal life.
> **MAIN CHARACTER.** What is eternal death?
> **CHRISTIAN.** The lake of fire is the second death, eternal death. If anyone's name is not found written in the book of life, he will be thrown into the lake of fire.
> **MAIN CHARACTER.** How does someone's name get written in that book?

CHRISTIAN. Anyone who calls on the name of the Lord shall be saved. So, you have to accept Jesus Christ as your Lord and Savior and make him the focal point of your life.

MAIN CHARACTER. What do I have to do to be saved?

CHRISTIAN. Just pray and tell Jesus that you know you're a sinner and that you are very sorry for it. Then ask him to come into your heart and to guide your life.

MAIN CHARACTER. What's next?

CHRISTIAN. Now you need to start reading the Bible to find out what God has for you.

Okay, so first you can see why I never broke into the entertainment business—pretty horrendous.

But more than that, despite the fact that statements "Christian" said can be matched to verses in the Bible, this explanation of the gospel is about the worst I've ever heard. It simply makes no sense. It isn't very effective in leading someone into a relationship with God.

NOTES

A Mindset for Sharing Our Faith

We know from the Bible that God wants us to "be a witness[13]" and to "do the work of an evangelist[14]." Yet, whenever I ask Christian groups if anyone feels ill-equipped to lead someone to salvation, there are always a few hands raised. I want to try and ease the internal conflict that Christians feel by sharing some simple thoughts on witnessing which are based on my own experiences over the last few years.

Since the most common obstacle to sharing our faith is fear, we need to address the cause of our fear. In my life, I can identify at least two main reasons why I've been afraid to talk to someone about Jesus: *I felt that I was on my own* and *I felt that I didn't know what to say.*

One of the most wonderful things about being a Christian is the fact that we're not alone. The Holy Spirit lives inside us. And it's not so much that he *helps* us to be a witness; he can actually speak *through* us when we talk to our friends.

"... [8]but you will receive power when the Holy Spirit has come upon you; and you shall be My witnesses both in Jerusalem, and in all Judea and Samaria, and even to the remotest part of the earth."

Acts 1:8

²⁰Therefore, we are ambassadors for Christ, as though God were making an appeal through us; we beg you on behalf of Christ, be reconciled to God.

2 Corinthians 5:20

Our part in witnessing isn't to manipulate a conversation with someone, but to yield ourselves to the Holy Spirit, who knows the perfect words for this person's heart. We'll speak the words that need to be spoken, and especially so, if we understand this key moment from Jesus' ministry.

It's more important for the listener to understand than for the speaker to speak.

In John 9, we read the story of Jesus healing a man who was born blind. The religious leaders of the day investigated the healed man's story (*interrogated* is more like it—both the man and his parents). We pick up the story in verse 24.

²⁴So a second time they called the man who had been born blind, and said to him, "Give glory to God; we know that this man [Jesus] is a sinner." ²⁵Then he answered, "Whether he is a sinner, I do not know; one thing I do know, that though I was blind, now I see."

John 9:24-25

Is that really true; the man had been healed, but didn't know whether or not Jesus was a sinner?

What this story shows us is that we don't have to know the theology of Jesus to know his interaction in our lives. Don't get me wrong. If we're his students, as Jesus said[15], we'll know his theology over time. But initially, what we must know is his involvement with us. *Though I was blind, now I see.* And once we've encountered him, we're qualified to tell others about it.

In order for us to *behave* like someone with a story to tell, we must *think* like someone with a message to share. We must become outreach-focused, being motivated by love for those who do not know God.

Our message is 'relationship with God,' 100%. So the first thing we must do is make sure our own relationship with God is growing. We should live with an expectancy to experience God. And because we want others to enjoy a relationship with God as well, we share stories of how this is happening in our lives. We influence people by both our lifestyle and our words.

Treating people with respect and dignity are the words that sum up our values, the way we must handle ourselves as we share. A relationship with God is a lifestyle that's different than what most people are familiar with. We aren't communicating that we're right and others are wrong. We're communicating that a relationship with God is right for everyone, and possible for anyone. One way we show respect is to not speak in cryptic Bible-talk, but in the language of those around us. *We gotta be down with it, ya'll.*

It's very important to build genuine friendships with people, building around common interests and shared experiences. We have to take this seriously because some people just don't want to be bothered with this God-stuff. They don't listen to people who thump them over the head with the Bible; they only listen to people they trust.

We all know people who'd rather not be bothered. Let's pray that God will soften their hardness. Let's pray that they won't be hurt by the hypocrisy of religion, but rather, that they will experience the love that comes from a relationship with God. Sometimes we would rather pray that God would let us off the hook and use someone else to talk with them. But instead, let's pray that God will keep us open to being used to share his message naturally and lovingly.

All people were created to experience a relationship with God. Peter wrote that it's not God's will for anyone to die without knowing him, but that all repent[16]. So, there's no reason not to pray.

First, We Share Our Stories

Let's let this be one of our guiding principles as we set ourselves to share our faith with others: *I will not allow myself to quote scripture to someone until I have shared my story first.* Shocking, isn't it?

It's true that the Bible is the inspired Word of God[17], the gospel is the power of God which results in salvation[18], and God's Word will prosper and accomplish what God wants[19]. But the question is: How powerful is scripture when the person we're talking to isn't interested? No one becomes a Christian against their will. The Word of God is astoundingly powerful, but only when someone is willing to listen.

Jesus said that we Christians are "the salt of the earth[20]." And one of the characteristics of salt is that it can make people thirsty. This means we can actually influence someone else in a way that can make them thirsty for God. And we do it the same way we cause people to be interested in a favorite restaurant or a good movie. We simply talk about our own positive experience.

To help see this in practical terms, we're going to work through a Q&A (question and answer) exercise together. I want us to answer each of the questions with brief sound bites. We're not looking to produce a polished writing suitable for publication; we're simply jotting down some notes.

I'll be sharing the testimonies of my ministry partners Sam and Brian, as well as my own, to demonstrate the principles involved.

❧ Describe the environment you grew up in?

....

....

....

Brian: I grew up in an alcoholic family. And that's what I did when I was old enough to do it, and probably before I was old enough to do it. I spent about ten years trying to see how annihilated I could get.

❧ How would you describe the person you were before you knew God?

....

....

....

Sam: I was a very greedy person. I was living by the law that says, "I'm going to stab you in the back before you have a chance to stab me. The way you get to the top: pile up enough bodies and you can climb there." That's seriously what I thought.

❧ At that time, what did you believe about God, the Bible, and Jesus? How did your beliefs affect your attitude, behavior, and relationships?

....

....

....

Sam: One of the things I had criticized most was these people who say, "God's telling me" blah, blah, blah. Whatever. I'm thinking, *Yeah right. I can make up better stories.*

☙ If you came to Jesus to have a desperate need met, what was it? If you had tried and failed to satisfy the need another way, describe the circumstances.

Brian: I couldn't take it anymore. I was suicidal. I came to work one night and, in a moment of what I considered weakness, I told my boss that I couldn't go on like I was. He reached out and set up a time for me to talk to a counselor. And that was my first step in the process of leaving that life behind, on the way to a better life.

I got involved with AA, a great program for people who have alcohol problems. I learned a lot. My relationship with God started then. And it was like I had my teenage years all over again. It was an awesome time for me.

I got married and had a couple of kids, but kind of wandered away from my relationship with God.

☙ In what ways did God use circumstances and/or other people to begin drawing you towards a relationship with him?

Sam: I got involved with, of all things, a network marketing company. And I kept hearing these guys talking 'my church, my church' all the time. I thought, *Wow, my wife goes to a church where there are ten thousand people.* Talk about plucking pigeons from the park, oh please.

I went to this church wearing a three-piece suit with a pistol under my coat. I was in the very last row, the very closest seat to the door, and I just sat there watching these people.

And this lady who had been singing says, "I have a word for somebody. God's telling me that you're stuck in the mire and muck, and that he's here to lift you up ..." Breaks me up even now.

Brian: After 15 years of marriage, I ended up going through a divorce. I went through another dark season in my life recovering from the divorce. But God was incredibly awesome through it all.

I was seeking God. I was involved in a church and had started reading my Bible. I waited until I was 40 years old to pick up the Bible and read it. But I had a hunger to know more about the things of God.

⚜ Specifically, what were the circumstances surrounding the moment you committed your life to Jesus?

....

....

....

Sam: I don't know what the guy preached. I sat there for 45 minutes and I couldn't get that woman's words out of my head. I just knew that God was pulling on me. And it was the first time that I really knew, without a shadow of a doubt, that there is a God.

And the guy says, "If God spoke to you, and you want to give yourself to Christ, raise your hand." So I raised my hand and put it back down. And he didn't see it. (laughs) My wife was about to have a fit next to me. I've still got bruised ribs. She says, "Raise your hand again." I looked at her and said, "It doesn't matter at this point." I started crying then and didn't stop for three months.

Eric: At the end of the sermon the evangelist asked us to come down to the front of the church if we wanted to accept salvation. My mom leaned over and asked me if I wanted to do that. I shook my head no because I was afraid of getting up in front of everyone. As I stood there, though, one thought kept going through my mind: *Now is your time.* After a few moments, I made a decision and tugged on Mom's dress.

Dad led me by the hand down the aisle to where one of the church elders was waiting to pray with people. He was cautious because of my young age—I was only five and a half—and asked, "Do you know why you've come forward?"

"To invite Jesus into my heart," I remember saying matter-of-factly.

A few moments later we were in a tiny prayer room. The elder was reading scriptures to me and asking if I believed what they said. My answer to each question was yes. I barely remember my prayer with him. But what I do remember clearly was the slightly panicked search for safety pins as they dressed my small body for baptism.

Meanwhile, there was a man towards the back of the church sitting with the friends he had come with. He was completely put off by the message of the gospel and had decided to reject Christ. He told God never to bother him with the salvation message again. As the curtains over the baptismal tank opened, he saw a young boy being baptized, and the Holy Spirit spoke to him.

If a child can see his need for Christ, why can't you?

With tears falling from his cheeks, he stood up and made his way to the front of the church.

I remember him being with us after the service was dismissed, as all of us who had accepted Christ that night met in the pastor's office to share the Lord's Supper together. And I remember the overwhelming joy inside me as I kept telling my parents on the way home, "I'm saved. I'm actually saved."

🙢 What has been the result of beginning your friendship with God?

Sam: I read the Bible, cover to cover, in three months. I had criticized it for 28 years and I decided that I might want to see what it says.

Brian: I've never felt so comforted, even in the midst of all those trials. He proved to me that he loves me. He proved to me that he could care for me. And he's made a huge difference in my life. My focus in life has changed. And it's more of an adventure today. It's just incredible what he did to my heart. I'm grateful for that, and I want to share that with as many people as I can.

Now that we've finished "jotting down some notes" for this exercise, try this. Go back to page 179 and read through your handwritten notes out loud. What you'll be reading is the basis of your salvation testimony. Sometime, try developing a 30-second *bullet point* version of your testimony and a 3-minute *story* version. Also, you may want to polish up your testimony for publication ... or at least for sharing with friends.

What God Has Done in My Life   Story A

When we Christians talk about our 'testimony,' we automatically think that we're *only* talking about the moment we received salvation. For me that was more than 37 years ago. If I really began a friendship with God way back when, then there should *also* be some stories of God's involvement in my life. These stories are also my testimony.

We're going to work through another Q&A (the second of three), this time focusing on healthy experiences that we've had, experiences that actually suggest that we've been born again and enjoy a personal friendship with God.

What follows are three columns of spiritual characteristics that can be experienced by Christians. Let's spend a few moments looking over the list, then we'll (circle) three of them that we've experienced personally in our lives.

God's Peace	The fruit of Love[21]	The gift of Wisdom[22]
God's Forgiveness	The fruit of Joy	The gift of Knowledge
God's Presence	The fruit of Patience	The gift of Healing
God's Voice	The fruit of Goodness	The gift of Prophecy
God's Comfort	The fruit of Gentleness	The gift of Discernment
God's Provision	The fruit of Self-Control	The gift of Tongues

We're just scratching the surface of everything that God says and does in the lives of people, and this list certainly isn't comprehensive. So before we actually begin this Q&A exercise, I want us to also choose three of the following 18 questions that we could answer with a specific situation from our own life.

- Has God given me direction when I had a difficult decision to make?
- Has God revealed his presence during a painful time in my life?
- Has God healed my physical body or given me patient endurance during a time of illness?
- Has God brought me recovery from a personal crisis?
- Has God broken the power of addiction in my life?
- Has God given me power to walk away from temptation?
- Has God kept me from harm and danger?
- Has God protected me when false accusations were made against me?
- Has God restored or strengthened my marriage or family relationships?

- Has God redirected my career or finances?
- Has God changed my morals and my perspective in life?
- Has God changed my understanding of himself, his church, or me?
- Has God used other people to help develop my faith?
- Has God shown me a new perspective on truth which I would consider life-changing?
- Has God renewed broken dreams, according to his purposes?
- Has God given me the strength to stand when my faith was challenged?
- Has God orchestrated a turning point in my life?
- Has God built monuments out of the ruins in my life?

Okay. So we've identified three characteristics and three situations we've experienced. We have six items to choose from as we prepare to develop a testimony from our friendship with God. Now, to give us all the freedom we need; if there's something else that God has said or done that we feel we should write about, we'll choose that. Otherwise, let's choose one of the first six items and proceed through the following questions.

꙯ Name the characteristic or situation you chose.

_____

꙯ Describe the way life was before you experienced God in this manner.

_____

_____

_____

꙯ In what ways did God use circumstances and/or other people to begin drawing you towards this experience with him?

_____

_____

_____

ﾐﾟ Specifically, what were the circumstances surrounding the moment God revealed himself through this experience?

_____

_____

_____

ﾐﾟ What has the impact of this experience been in your life?

_____

_____

_____

Again, we've finished "jotting down some notes" for a testimony. As you read through these handwritten notes out loud, you'll be reading a simple story of God's work in your life. I would suggest that you polish up this testimony to share with people, too.

Then, We Present God's Story

I said earlier that we shouldn't allow ourselves to quote scripture until we've shared our story. Now let me say that if we are going to tell our story, we need to be committed to quoting scripture when the appropriate time does come.

This is where we Christians tend to freak out. But at some point, it becomes necessary for us to move from our stories and our concern to scripture. Their story isn't going to be one of our stories, but the Word of God *is* going to be the Word of God for them. Sharing God's story becomes the most appropriate thing to do.

I'm not suggesting that we learn ancient languages. We don't have to explain Bible concepts like *propitiation* to someone. In no way do we have to be scholars. Even so, I would guess we know more than we think we do.

We're about to work through our third and final Q&A exercise, which will help us see what we've already learned from the *8 Great Wonders*. We'll capture the essence of Chapter 7 through Chapter 11 in just a sentence or two. Actually, we've already had a chance to do this. Does this sound familiar? ***Important:***

Your written notes here will be used in an exercise later in the book. Guess what; it's later. We can simply copy what we wrote at the conclusion of the past several chapters.

Story **B**

The Gospel: Relationship Is Intended

☙ Taken at face value, what implications does the headline **God Creates People** have for the entire human race? (see page 99)

_____

_____

_____

We were created to be like God. We are meant to be with him.

Story **C**

The Gospel: Salvation Is Necessary—Part One

☙ Taken at face value, what implications does the headline **People Sin Against God** have for the entire human race? (see page 116)

_____

_____

_____

Sin separated the human race from God. It still makes God seem distant.

Story **D**

The Gospel: Salvation Is Necessary—Part Two

☙ Taken at face value, what implications does the headline **God's Law Is Given** have for the entire human race? (see page 134)

_____

_____

_____

The Law condemned us all to die as sinners. It still makes us feel guilty.

The Gospel: Salvation Is Provided—Part One   Story **E**

⤷ Taken at face value, what implications does the headline **Jesus Christ Dies** have for the entire human race? (see page 149)

....

....

....

We died with Jesus when he died for us. God forgave and reconciled us.

The Gospel: Salvation Is Provided—Part Two   Story **F**

⤷ Taken at face value, what implications does the headline **Jesus, Alive Again** have for the entire human race? (see page 169)

....

....

....

Jesus was raised from the dead. He offers all of us life from the dead.

I said before that one of the fears that we may face is thinking that we don't really know what to say. Even when we are able to share our own stories, we're somehow convinced that we don't know how to communicate the message of the gospel properly. But, look at all of our answers on these pages. The gospel is staring us right in the face ... and it came from our own pens.

This is a great moment for a lot of Christians, a real turning point. They didn't know that they actually do know the gospel.

A B C D E F G

Now, let me explain how we can use all of these Q&A exercises to help draw others into a relationship with God.

We said that "our message is 'relationship with God,' 100%." Because we want others to enjoy a relationship with God as well, we share stories of how this is happening in our own lives. Story $\boxed{\text{A}}$, *What God Has Done in My Life*, is what we communicate to others consistently.

Today we share the story that we wrote on pages 184-185. Tomorrow, it's the story behind one of the other five experiences we could have chosen. With our neighbor, we share our experience of God's comfort. We tell our friend how God has restored or strengthened our marriage or family relationships. See how this works? We're always sharing our 'relationship' testimonies.

Everything about our stories points to God's intervention in our lives. We want people to begin seeing how God works, so that they will begin to wonder if he'll work the same way in their life. We want people to know that what Christ has done for us he can do for them.

One day, you'll hear something similar to what my friend Craig told me. "This sounds completely crazy, but when you say that God talks to you, that you have a relationship with him, I believe you. I really do. But it brings up a nagging question. Why hasn't God ever spoken to me?"

The answer is as simple as $\boxed{\text{B}}$ $\boxed{\text{C}}$ $\boxed{\text{D}}$ $\boxed{\text{E}}$ $\boxed{\text{F}}$ and $\boxed{\text{G}}$.

With respect and dignity, we share Stories $\boxed{\text{B}}$ through $\boxed{\text{F}}$, *The Gospel*. We tell our friend that a relationship with God is right for everyone, and through Jesus Christ, it's possible for anyone. We quote scriptures and paraphrase stories from God's Word to support the message that God loves us and wants us to be born again, that God wants us to know him personally.

As we finish talking about Jesus' resurrection and his offer to raise us to life spiritually, we make it personal once again. We share Story $\boxed{\text{G}}$, *When I Accepted Salvation*. Maybe it sounds something like this:

You know, I grew up in an alcoholic family, and I was a very greedy person. I criticized people who say, 'God's telling me' blah, blah, blah.

But I couldn't take it anymore. And this lady says, 'I have a word for somebody. God's telling me that you're stuck in the mire and muck, and he's here to lift you up.' It was the first time that I really knew that there is a God.

'If God spoke to you, and you want to give yourself to Christ, raise your hand.' So I raised my hand. A few moments later we were in a prayer room reading scriptures. They asked if I believed what they said.

Do you believe what I've told you about Jesus? Would you like to begin a friendship with God?

Now, here's the hard part. The decision is completely theirs. We're responsible to share our stories and to invite them in, but not for their response.

I remember seeing tears in the eyes of each of my friends Scott and Craig, who I've talked about in this book, when I asked them this important question. I said, "You feel God tugging on your heart, don't you?"

In each case, they nodded.

"I want us to pray together, but I'm not going to tell you what to pray. You know what's in your heart and on your mind. I want you to talk to God for just a few of moments and tell him what you're feeling. Tell him what you expect him to do in your life."

A 'repeat-after-me' prayer for salvation can be great for those who are too overwhelmed or too unsure to pray on their own.

As a result of leading people in this way, I've heard the most beautiful and heart-felt prayers for salvation.

I like to end these times with a brief prayer of my own as well; basically the prayer on page 56 in the section called *Celebration for a Life*.

These are important moments. Jesus said that there's joyful celebration in heaven when moments like these take place[23].

Does leading your friends to this moment still seem intimidating? Here's a final suggestion that might help.

Let other people tell the stories for you. We're not limited to using our own stories. We can share what God has done in the lives of other people. Maybe this means we open up a Christian magazine and point out a few stories to a friend or visit a Christian 'testimony' Internet site with someone. I know a woman who hands out printed copies of her testimony to people she meets. Why couldn't we hand out her story, too? Or better yet, write out our own story?

We're not limited to our own presentation of salvation scriptures either. Why wouldn't we want to keep a few gospel tracts in our pockets? My uncle used to stock me up with tracts almost every time I visited him. What could be easier than pointing to the plan of salvation on glossy paper, or logging on to a Christian ministry web site that features a presentation of the gospel?

There's no reason to limit ourselves with the thought *I have to do all this by myself*, especially when we realize that it isn't about us anyway. It's God's love, God's plan, and God's message in the hands of the Holy Spirit that brings people into a relationship with Jesus Christ.

We're just the messengers.

The Extra Effort (Search & Rescue)

☙ *your name Accepts Salvation*—Why does it matter? Taken at face value, what implications does this headline have for the entire human race?

_____

_____

_____

☙ *your name Accepts Salvation*—What difference does it make for you? Think about these statements and summarize your response below.
- I have been born again.
- I understand the imperative for me to share my personal stories of faith until others become interested.
- I can share the gospel message once someone is interested.

_____

_____

_____

* * *

☙ If you can, note a recent news story, as well as a personal story, that relates to topics in this chapter.

News: _____

Personal: _____

᠊ᢙ List two things that impacted you as you read the chapter or participated in a group discussion.

....

....

....

Scoring for *Search & Rescue* discussion groups:

Read-4 ∗ *Notes-8* ∗ *News-1* ∗ *Personal-2* ∗ *Impact-16* ∗ *Total-_____*

1 Acts 2:11

2 Acts 2:41

3 Acts 5:14

4 Acts 6:7

5 Acts 8:9-13

6 Acts 8:26-39

7 Acts 9:1-22

8 Acts 10:1-48

9 Acts 13:6-12

10 Acts 16:14-15

11 Acts 16:23-34

12 Acts 18:8

13 Acts 1:8

14 2 Timothy 4:5

15 John 8:31-32

16 2 Peter 3:9

17 2 Timothy 3:16

18 Romans 1:16

19 Isaiah 55:10-11

20 Matthew 5:13

21 Galatians 5:22-23

22 1 Corinthians 12:8-11

23 Luke 15:10

your name LIVES BY FAITH

*** Family, friends, neighbors, co-workers impacted by one person's life-change ***

editorial— How many George Bailey's do you know? George Bailey, of course, is the name of the central character in the movie *It's a Wonderful Life*. George's sense of personal purpose was second only to his willingness to put others ahead of himself. I've been asking myself lately, "What makes a good Christian?" The

more I think about it the more George Bailey's name comes to mind. So who is it that you know *personally* who exhibits a strong sense of personal purpose and vision? Who do you know who is willing, maybe even driven, to put the interests of other people ahead of their own? There is, of course, something more to being a

good Christian than just being a servant-leader. Ask yourself, does the George (or Georgette) Bailey I know follow the direct leading of God in his or her life? If so, your friend is an example of a good Christian, with a wonderful life. Are you?

Related Story

—Acts, chapters 3 through 5

13 ❧ <u>your name</u> Lives by Faith

I Love This Song

In the last chapter we said that our message, 100%, is 'relationship with God,' so we want to make sure that our own friendship with God is growing. That's what this chapter is all about.

I want to begin with an analogy that's one of the best I've ever heard in describing a relationship, as well as a non-relationship, with God.

Think about your favorite song for a moment.

It just so happens, this is the song we hear playing in a room just down the hallway from here. You and I walk down the hall, we poke our heads into the doorway, and we see two people in the room. They're both snapping their fingers and tapping their toes. "Ah, they're listening to my favorite song."

The longer we watch these two individuals the more we begin to notice that the first person is not only snapping and tapping, but he's moving his head back and forth with his eyes closed. We can tell that he's really feeling the music. The second person, we notice, seems to watch the first person's snapping fingers and tapping toes ... *a lot*.

The first person stops snapping and tapping right as the song ends. But the second person stops after an extra beat. *What's up with this?* As the first person's hands begin to move in words of sign language, we realize that the second person is deaf. He hasn't heard the song at all. He's only been imitating the snaps and taps of his friend.

There are two ways to live as a Christian. One is to be in a personal, intimate relationship with God; through Jesus Christ, through the Holy Spirit. God communicates with us. He speaks to us. Our life is a response to the music we hear. The second way is to follow what we see in the lives of Christians around us. They read the Bible; *Okay, I'll read the Bible.* They attend church; we attend church. What we're actually doing is imitating the actions of Christianity without hearing the music of God's voice.

After we understand that life is all about hearing the music of his voice, and once we begin to hear the music for ourselves, then it's valid to take a look around at what's happening with Christians around us. We can actually gain something valuable for our own lives then.

I was asked to speak at a Wednesday night church service. The pastor gave me the assignment of showing others what the Christian life can look like, and he told me to use stories from my own life to do it.

"You've got to be kidding. My life isn't perfect."

The pastor chuckled and said, "Everybody knows that nobody's perfect. But there *are* moments in our lives which turn out to be pretty decent moments with God. I want you to share a few of your moments like this."

It also helped a lot when he reminded me that Paul wrote, "Imitate me, just like I imitate Christ[1]."

What follows are three pretty decent moments from my life with God. I've talked about these stories many times, probably more times than any other experiences I've had.

"Apologize to Jennifer."

I started a new job a number of years ago, and, unfortunately, I got off on the wrong foot with my supervisor. Her name was Jennifer. Three months into it, I was firmly convinced that this job couldn't possibly be what God wanted for my life, so I decided that I would look for a new job and then quit.

The next morning I woke up and the very first thought which came into my mind was this: *Apologize to Jennifer.*

God himself had spoken to me. I know it was God because my next thought was: *You've got to be kidding me. I haven't done anything wrong.*

Part III: Follow the Path

Here's the funny thing about arguing with God. He doesn't participate. He had simply told me to apologize to Jennifer and then gave me a sense of knowing that this was exactly what he wanted me to do—period.

Between this thought and getting to work, I spent the entire time telling God, sometimes out loud, "I can't believe you're making me do this."

But, I had made a decision earlier in my life that I would do whatever God told me to do. And I was committed to following through on that.

I got to work and met Jennifer at her desk. "I know that things have been fairly tense between us, and I just wanted to apologize for my part in all that. Please forgive me."

I'll never forget her response. "There's an urgent matter on your desk. You need to go and take care of it." She didn't even acknowledge my apology!

So I walked to my work area, looking up to the ceiling, thinking, *God, I did what you told me to do, and it didn't work. It's in your hands now.*

Later, Jennifer came over to evaluate my work. (Like I said, it had been three months—job benefits were about to kick in.) I don't know what happened exactly, but there was tension almost immediately.

Jennifer told me we needed to talk and took me into a conference room. Quite honestly, she did a couple of amazing things.

This was the first. She told me that I could say anything I felt I needed to say to her, and that she wouldn't hold it against me. I found her words difficult to believe, but I was planning to quit anyway, so what did I have to lose? I, very politely and professionally, shared some things which I thought were issues between us. Then, she also took the opportunity to tell me a few things which she felt she needed to say.

When we finished the conversation, she did the second amazing thing. She said, "Now that we've talked, you and I are friends." I didn't say anything, but I didn't believe it was possible.

To my surprise, she began to pull it off. She began speaking to me with a smile. And it didn't seem to be a big effort on her part.

One day Jennifer came to my work station and said, "Eric, I've got a Bible question for you." I was completely surprised. But this wasn't the only time it happened. She asked me questions about the Bible every few days for a couple of weeks. And each time I would give her whatever answer I could.

One morning she came to me with a big smile on her face. "Eric, you'll never guess what happened to me last night. I prayed to accept Jesus as my Lord and Savior."

At that very moment I knew exactly what "Apologize to Jennifer" really meant. It had less to do with problems at work, and more to do with a woman finding some answers to her questions about God, and ultimately, finding *the* answer—Jesus Christ.

NOTES

"Keep going."

My desire is to pray and read the Bible in the morning, before anyone else wakes up. One morning I opened my Bible, not sure of what I wanted to read that day. I had finished reading the Book of Acts the day before. I could start Romans, the next book in the New Testament, but I wanted to read something different. I asked the Holy Spirit, "Where would you like me to read?" I didn't 'hear anything' per se, but I just sensed *Proverbs*, so I turned to the Book of Proverbs in the Old Testament.

My usual practice is to read two or three chapters each morning. When I finished Chapter 3, I started to close my Bible ... but it felt as if the Holy Spirit said, *Keep going*.

So I read Chapter 4. Again, *Keep going*.

Then I read Chapter 5. *Keep going*.

I read Chapter 6. When I was done, I waited on the Holy Spirit a moment or two, and it felt as if I was done.

Now, I want you to know that nothing was really jumping off the pages at me. I read and reread a couple of verses in a couple of places, but nothing was hitting me. No lightning bolts of any kind.

I was at work later that day. Sometime during the morning, my UPS driver came in and said, "Eric, I've got a really important Bible question for you." He was going through some pretty tough times at home: betrayal, adultery, anger, divorce. "I want you to go home tonight, read this scripture, and then tell me tomorrow what it means."

"Okay, which one is it?"

"It's a verse in Proverbs 6."

I smiled. "Which verse is it specifically?"

"There's a verse that says if a man commits adultery with another man's wife, then the husband's going to be outraged[2]. And it's like setting yourself on fire[3]. Is God telling me that I have a right to beat the you-know-what out of that you-know who?"

"No, no! That's not what God is saying."

We talked for several minutes and I think I was able to help him ... and maybe even 'you-know-who' as well.

The job I had when I talked with my UPS driver, when I worked for Jennifer—the job I thought I would leave after 90 days—ended up lasting nine years. Obviously, it was exactly what God wanted for my life during that time. And the most dramatic proof of that, to me anyway, comes from my friendship with a woman named Rosie.

Rosie worked in our satellite office in Southern California. Our business relationship, as well as our friendship, pretty much developed over the phone. Rosie was a Christian who talked a lot about her church family, and about her son Tony and her daughter Cathy. And she was always asking me about my wife and little daughter. We would laugh a lot, and every now and then one of us would remember that we called with a work-related issue.

On a Monday morning in October, 2002, I learned that my friend Rosie had been assaulted and killed in her car; the victim of an apparent random act.

My immediate thoughts were for Rosie's children and church family. I kept picturing myself being there to help them through this. But I was in Kansas and they were 1,500 miles away.

Later in the day, the company owners offered those of us who knew Rosie best the opportunity to attend her funeral, paying for our airline tickets and hotel reservations. I was amazed that what I couldn't stop thinking about was actually going to take place.

Then something interesting began happening. Over the next couple of days, five different people said things like, "You're going to California on a mission, aren't you?" and "God's got you going for a reason, doesn't he?"

One woman, who wasn't really known for being religious, said, "Are you going to be speaking at the funeral? It would be great if you did."

Scratching my head, I began asking God, *Am I?*

I remembered the night I refused to stand up and stop a false prophet. My recommitment to God from that night began to echo in my mind: *From now on I'll do whatever you ask me to do. I'll never disobey you again.*

Alright, God, if I am going for a purpose, then I'm counting on hearing from you. I'll do whatever you ask me to do.

My flight to Los Angeles was scheduled for early Friday afternoon, but I was also registered for a church conference that began Friday morning. I decided to go ahead and attend the first few hours of the conference. Right before I absolutely had to leave for the airport, they offered attendees an opportunity to be prayed for by local church leaders.

I went up and was met by a young man who asked how he could pray for me. Briefly, I shared the story of Rosie and my trip to LA. Then he prayed in regard to everything I mentioned, *and* for something I didn't.

He prayed, "Lord, I ask you to give Eric the boldness to do what you've asked him to do on the plane."

I had only told my wife that God was telling me to let the two co-workers I would be traveling with—both Christians—know about God's purposes for the trip, and to tell them to be ready as well. After the young man prayed, I was no longer wondering if God was really speaking to me about it.

I talked to my two 'fellow missionaries' on the plane that afternoon and they were both excited to see what God might have for us to do.

One of the company owners picked us up at LAX and we were shuttled directly to Rosie's wake in Santa Ana.

The chapel was full of friends, family, and business associates. I met and embraced members of Rosie's church, and then I was introduced to Tony and Cathy. Both teenagers reacted as if they already knew me. I had never seen such emptiness in anyone's eyes. My heart broke. I had never experienced anyone mourning as deeply as Cathy was. I can't even put it into words.

I prayed for Cathy and Tony a zillion times during the service. I was alert to everything around me, but God didn't speak beyond my own compassion that night.

We arrived at the cemetery Saturday morning to a long line of people waiting to go into the chapel. Outside, in the misty rain, I couldn't help but thank God for the miracle of the airline tickets and hotel reservation. *I wanted so much to be here for Rosie's family.* I saw Rosie's daughter as I walked up the steps, and God said to me, *Tell Cathy she'll smile again.*

As Cathy and I hugged one another I whispered God's message into her ear. And for a brief moment she did smile, but the look on her face immediately melted into sorrow again.

I found a seat with my co-workers and prayed a thank-you prayer. *Lord, I'm okay if that's what the trip was about because I know that I've heard you, and I know that one day what you spoke, will happen—Cathy will smile again. Thank you for your message of hope.*

The funeral began with beautiful music and prayers. Then, they invited anyone who wanted to say a few words to come and do so.

The Holy Spirit said, *You're speaking next.*

My heart pounded. One of my legs shook uncontrollably. *God, there's 300 people here!*

I had no clue what I was going to say. And I was halfway up to the pulpit before I realized that I was ... actually walking up to the pulpit.

Once I stood and faced the people, my mouth opened:

"My name is Eric. I was a business associate of Rosie's for the last six years of her life."

I literally felt as if I was listening just like everyone else in the room.

"I don't want to repeat all the things that have already been said about Rosie. I know that her faith in Jesus Christ was strong, and that she cherished her daughter Cathy and her son Tony.

"I don't want to presume to speak for God, but I believe I have a message from the Lord for Cathy and Tony, and the rest of us as well.

"Cathy, when I walked in and we embraced this morning, I said that you will smile again. I want you to know that this message comes directly from the heart of God. You will smile again."

I turned to Tony, who stood with his entire high school football team, dressed out in their jerseys.

"Tony, your mother worked hard to give you the best life she could. The Lord wants you to know that it's now your responsibility to go out and get that life, the life she wanted for you. You're responsible now to go out and get it.

"It's wonderful to see that you're a part of a team with all of these young men here this morning."

I turned to the rest of the mourners.

"We're all a team. We're a family and we need to help one another get through this.

"Because of the circumstances of Rosie's death, there's a great temptation to focus our attention on justice, vengeance, and punishment. Let's leave justice in the hands of law enforcement and the legal system. Let's learn the lessons from Rosie's life. Let's cherish our families and strengthen our faith in God.

"Thank you."

I walked back to my seat. The company owner who had flown us to California hugged me. She said, "There couldn't have been any words spoken more perfect than those. I'm so proud of you."

I sat there thanking God for those perfect words ... while trying desperately to remember exactly what they were.

A Review in Sound Bites

Christian bookstores and pastors' libraries are jam-packed with books on how to live as a Christian.

With a golf pencil and a few 3x5 cards in my hands I walked the aisles of a local Christian bookstore, making a list of all the areas of spiritual life and service that I could identify from the book titles. When I had finished my informal, unscientific search, I had found 85 different areas.

Memorize Bible verses. Give 10% of your income to God's work.
Lift holy hands in praise. Express perfect character traits.
Teach Bible studies. Hand out gospel tracts.
Support foreign orphanages. Visit the sick. Drive the church bus.
Sing hymns on key. Recite the Sermon on the Mount backwards.

You know, there's nothing wrong with Christian activity—except maybe that 'backwards sermon' one. But being a Christian isn't about setting a routine of activities. It's not at all about imitating the snapping fingers and tapping toes of Christians around us.

If we decide that we want to hear the music of heaven and dance, then there's only one thing that we need to focus on—our personal relationship with God.

What follows is a series of 'relationship' sound bites, pulled from the previous chapters of this book. I believe that these statements lay the groundwork for our discussion in this chapter.

* * *

We've heard that *Christianity is a relationship, not a religion.*

Although many of us have heard the phrase *relationship with God*, few of us have been told what it means.

Does the word *relationship*, when applied to God and me, mean the same thing as when it's applied to marriage, friendships, or even neighbors?

Relationship consists of mutual respect, communication, and shared experiences that have drawn us closer personally.

'Relationship with God' actually means *friendship*, not *religion*.

This relationship is revealed through God's history with people.

A picture of the health and wholeness that comes from a personal relationship with God is a picture of God the Father, Jesus Christ, and the Holy Spirit ... *connected to* ... a person's spirit, soul, and body.

We're not born into this world already experiencing a relationship with God. It doesn't happen automatically.

There's no such thing as a completely whole person outside of a relationship with God. And there's no such thing as a relationship with God unless our spirit is born again.

Dead people need life. Live people need relationship. All people need Jesus—period.

The question of 'relationship' is what reveals our greatest need.

A relationship with God is a lifestyle that's different than what most people are familiar with. We aren't communicating that we're right and others are wrong. We're communicating that a relationship with God is right for everyone, and possible for anyone.

Rather than feeling separated from him, we can experience a reconciled relationship. Rather than thinking that we are condemned, we can know God's forgiveness and grace ... once we've dealt with the issue of our death.

What is Faith?

NOTES

The title of this chapter is <u>your name</u> Lives by Faith. And the theme of the *8 Great Wonders* message is 'relationship with God.' Faith and our friendship with God are connected. I'm convinced that if we understand the dynamic of faith in our lives, then relationship becomes incredibly simple. So let's talk about faith.

If we were to ask pastors what faith is, the most common answer we would hear would be, "Hebrews 11:1."

¹Now faith is the assurance of things hoped for, the conviction of things not seen.
Hebrews 11:1

Now this scripture is certainly true, but I want us to be honest and ask ourselves a question. Are we any closer to understanding faith now than we were a few minutes ago? What if someone said this?

Now running shoes are the key to a sprinter's ability to win races, the reason Maurice Green set a World Record.

It's a true enough statement, but we could still walk right past a pair of running shoes and not know them when we see them. What do they look like? How are they properly used? Do they come in our size?

your name Lives by Faith   203

Although the first verse of Hebrews 11 doesn't fully explain what faith is, we can learn a lot by looking at the entire chapter.

I've mentioned the story of how my religious beliefs took a direct hit the day my dad was rushed to the emergency room. Our family believed that it's *always* God's will to heal his people of sickness and disease. Even though my response was to pray, "Something has gone wrong, God. Show me the truth," the answers didn't come overnight. Dad was in the Intensive Care Unit for four months. And they were long months, filled with questions.

During this time, my wife and I played hooky from church one Sunday morning. Actually, it was a little more serious than that. Because of Dad's crisis, we needed answers, and God had led both of us to a study of Hebrews 11.

Here's what we did. Out loud, Francine read a verse or two from Hebrews that spoke about the faith of a particular Old Testament person. Then, I read the full story from the Old Testament that was mentioned. We began to see the definition of faith as we compared the similarities in these stories.

The Faith of Noah

7By faith Noah, being warned by God about things not yet seen, in reverence prepared an ark for the salvation of his household, by which he condemned the world, and became an heir of the righteousness which is according to faith.

Hebrews 11:7

13Then God said to Noah, "The end of all flesh has come before Me; for the earth is filled with violence because of them; and behold, I am about to destroy them with the earth. 14Make for yourself an ark of gopher wood; ..."

Genesis 6:13-14a

the story concludes ...

22Thus Noah did; according to all that God had commanded him, so he did.

Genesis 6:22

The Faith of Abraham

8By faith Abraham, when he was called, obeyed by going out to a place which he was to receive for an inheritance; and he went out, not knowing where he was going.

Hebrews 11:8

1Now the Lord said to Abram,
"Go forth from your country,
And from your relatives

And from your father's house,

To the land which I will show you;

²And I will make you a great nation,

And I will bless you,

And make your name great;

And so you shall be a blessing;

³And I will bless those who bless you,

And the one who curses you I will curse.

And in you all the families of the earth will be blessed."

⁴So Abram went forth as the Lord had spoken to him; ...   *Genesis 12:1-4a*

The Faith of Moses

²⁹By faith they passed through the Red Sea as though they were passing through dry land; ...   *Hebrews 11:29a*

¹⁵Then the Lord said to Moses, "Why are you crying out to Me? Tell the sons of Israel to go forward. ¹⁶As for you, lift up your staff and stretch out your hand over the sea and divide it, and the sons of Israel shall go through the midst of the sea on dry land."   *Exodus 14:15-16*

the story concludes ...

²¹Then Moses stretched out his hand over the sea; and the Lord swept the sea back by a strong east wind all night and turned the sea into dry land, so the waters were divided. ²²The sons of Israel went through the midst of the sea on the dry land, and the waters were like a wall to them on their right hand and on their left.   *Exodus 14:21-22*

The Faith of Joshua

³⁰By faith the walls of Jericho fell down after they had been encircled for seven days.   *Hebrews 11:30*

²The Lord said to Joshua, "See, I have given Jericho into your hand, with its king and the valiant warriors. ³You shall march around the city, all the men of war circling the city once. You shall do so for six days. ⁴Also seven priests shall carry seven trumpets of rams' horns before the ark; then on the seventh day you shall march around the city seven times, and the priests shall blow the trumpets. ⁵It shall be that when they make a long blast with the ram's horn, and when you hear the sound of the trumpet, all the people shall shout with a great shout; and

the wall of the city will fall down flat, and the people will go up every man
straight ahead."

Joshua 6:2-5

the story concludes ...

¹⁴... they marched around the city once and returned to the camp; they did so for
six days.

¹⁵Then on the seventh day they rose early at the dawning of the day and
marched around the city in the same manner seven times; only on that day they
marched around the city seven times. ¹⁶At the seventh time, when the priests
blew the trumpets, Joshua said to the people, "Shout! For the Lord has given you
the city."

Joshua 6:14b-16

Are we closer to understanding faith *now*?

Another verse from Hebrews refers to Jesus as "the author and finisher of our faith[4]." In essence, faith begins and ends with him. And that's exactly what my wife and I saw in our study of Hebrews 11 that Sunday morning.

Each summary in Hebrews begins with the words "by faith." The Old Testament stories begin with, "The Lord God said," followed by the belief and obedience of God's servant, which resulted in God's miraculous blessing. So, here's what we discovered.

Faith is a response of belief and obedience to what God initiates in a
person's life. Faith allows us to experience his will for our lives.

For a time, I was offering 10-minute devotional talks to a group of home-schooled students. One morning I taught them that faith is *The BOB Principle* (**B**elief + **O**bedience = **B**lessing).

Now that faith is defined, Hebrews 11:1 makes more sense to us. "Faith (obedience) is the assurance of things hoped for (God's intervention). Faith (belief) is the conviction of things not seen (God's initiative in my spirit)."

When I talk about God's initiative or hearing from God, I'm talking specifically about the Holy Spirit communicating with our spirit. We've seen that when we are born again, our spirit is brought to life and the Holy Spirit comes to live inside us. So when God speaks to us, he is speaking by the Holy Spirit.

¹⁰For to us God revealed [the things he has prepared for us] *through the Spirit;*
for the Spirit searches all things, even the depths of God. ¹¹For who among men
knows the thoughts of a man except the spirit of the man which is in him? Even
so the thoughts of God no one knows except the Spirit of God. ¹²Now we have
received, not the spirit of the world, but the Spirit who is from God, so that we
may know the things freely given to us by God, ¹³which things we also speak,

not in words taught by human wisdom, but in those taught by the Spirit,
combining spiritual thoughts with spiritual words.   *1 Corinthians 2:10-13*

[Jesus said,] *26"But the Helper, the Holy Spirit, whom the Father will send in My*
name, He will teach you all things, and bring to your remembrance all that I
said to you."   *John 14:26*

The Holy Spirit tells us to do specific things.

2While they were ministering to the Lord and fasting, the Holy Spirit said, "Set
apart for Me Barnabas and Saul for the work to which I have called them."
3Then, when they had fasted and prayed and laid their hands on them, they sent
them away.   *Acts 13:2-3*

The Holy Spirit tells us *not* to do other things.

6They passed through the Phrygian and Galatian region, having been
forbidden by the Holy Spirit to speak the word in Asia; ...   *Acts 16:6*

And the Holy Spirit can bring a sense of confirmation to things we discuss with other maturing Christians.

28"For it seemed good to the Holy Spirit and to us to lay upon you no greater
burden than these essentials: ..."   *Acts 15:28*

Here's the key to hearing the voice of the Holy Spirit. We don't have to sit on the couch, watching TV, waiting for the Holy Spirit to speak to us. *God knows where to find me if he ever needs me.*

Light from heaven doesn't shine down with a voice that says, "It is time for me to speaketh to thee."

Instead, I've found that the Holy Spirit's favorite time to speak is when I'm reading the Bible. "Faith comes by hearing [God]," Paul wrote, "and hearing [God] comes by the Word of God.5"

So we open the Bible and we pray for the Holy Spirit to teach us, to speak to us, to meet us in our need. Because of this, we have a say-so in how our friendship with God develops.

Here's the question; what could it look like if you and I took our say-so seriously and lived by faith, believing and obeying the voice of the Holy Spirit?

Time with God

You may remember *Birth, School, Work, Death* from Chapter 7, a list of different characteristics from God that can be experienced by a spirit that has been born again. We talked about mercy and forgiveness, encouragement, comfort, love, joy, peace, words of wisdom, the gift of healing, discernment, and much more.

In Chapter 12 we read through a list of questions concerning God's interaction in our lives. We saw questions like, "Has God broken the power of addiction?" and, "Has God changed my morals and my perspective in life?"

Each outcome those questions describe is a result of God's initiative in our lives, maybe the result of one of the characteristics specifically; 'his encouragement' 'renews broken dreams,' 'his power' 'breaks addictions,' 'his discernment' 'keeps us from harm.'

When the Holy Spirit expresses peace in us, the kind the Bible refers to as "the peace of God which is beyond our comprehension[6]," then we need to respond to that peace with belief and obedience. He wants us to have faith when peace comes into our heart. That means we have to fight for it when circumstances try to take it from us.

Faith also comes into play when we experience God's character or his promises to his children. When we see the faithfulness of God in our lives, then we should respond with the belief that God is faithful. We should live in a way that demonstrates that belief.

With all of this talk about *our* belief and *our* obedience, it might be easy for us to conclude that faith is completely under our control. But one of the gifts of the Spirit is something called *the gift of faith*. Does the Holy Spirit give people an ability to believe and obey? Sometimes. I may not know how to explain it, but I know that since it's a gift from the Holy Spirit, it doesn't come from me.

There was a desperate father who came to Jesus about his demon-possessed son. Jesus saw the terrible condition the boy was in and said, "Anything's possible if you believe.[7]" The father responded, "Lord, I believe; *help* my unbelief." The writer of Hebrews tells us that Jesus is the same yesterday, today, and forever[8]. He will respond the same way when we come to him *today* and say, "I believe; *help* my unbelief." He sees when we take those nervous steps toward him in obedience. He's there to help us with our faith.

It's much easier to talk about these things than to practice them in a crisis. It's also easier to try to help people in their understanding of these things when we're not going through it ourselves. It doesn't really become real for us until we experience it first hand.

I'd love to hand us the experience of time with God on a silver platter. But all I can really do is make a few suggestions and give us some space at the end of the chapter to journal what happens.

A one-time experience with God is good, but three experiences might be enough to get us into the practice of seeking God on an on-going basis. So, space is provided for three exercises.

In *Time with God #1,* we'll read scripture from the Old Testament; maybe a favorite Bible story, the Psalms, or Proverbs.

We'll read from the Gospels or the Book of Acts in *Time with God #2.* There's plenty for God to say from the life of Jesus and the birth of Christianity.

Finally, in *Time with God #3,* we'll focus on teaching from the New Testament Letters (Romans through Revelation).

Here's how I'd suggest we structure our *Time with God*:

- Let's set aside 30 to 45 minutes of uninterrupted time.
- As we begin, let's ask God to fill us with his Holy Spirit. And let's ask the Holy Spirit to speak to us, to teach us, to meet with us. Then, let's read the Bible for no less than 10 minutes. More is better.
- Afterwards, let's spend time thinking and praying about what we read, although we shouldn't limit God during this time. The Holy Spirit may want to talk about other issues in our life.

I think we'll find these exercises very rewarding, but be aware of this. There's going to be an incredible temptation to shrug them off and not do them. Remember, *when an individual gets too close to this "relationship with God" thing, Satan …*

Know this though. Over time, as we continue to approach God like this, and we hear and respond to what he is saying, something amazing happens.

From Faith to Faith

Paul said that God's righteousness is revealed from faith to faith[9]. That doesn't mean that Christianity is revealed from my faith to your faith to his faith to her faith. It means that God's character is revealed from my faith experience today to my faith experience tomorrow and on and on. What it means is that I get to know God a little bit more each time I respond to him with belief and obedience.

It gets better than that. Not only did Paul write that God's righteousness is revealed from faith to faith, but he also said that, in Christ, you and I have become the righteousness of God[10]. So, because of our faith, not only do we get to *experience* his righteousness, but we get to *become* his righteousness. Not only do we get to know him better, but we get to become a little more like him everyday. Specifically, we become more like Jesus.

> [29]*"For those whom* [God] *foreknew, He also predestined to become conformed to the image of His Son, ...*
>
> Romans 8:29

The Bible says that we will physically become like Jesus when we see him as he is[11]. We'll experience this 'body salvation' when he comes again. But this principle also applies to our lives here and now. When we see him for "who he is," we will become like him.

Take a moment for this to soak in. If we experience the forgiveness of Jesus, we can become more forgiving. If we experience the generosity of Jesus, we can become more generous. And all of this will happen as faith is taking place in our lives on an on-going basis.

What we're talking about is the fact that the Holy Spirit develops our character "from faith to faith."

Jesus modeled faith for us. John wrote that Jesus told people on at least seven different occasions[12] that his Father in heaven initiated everything he said and did. And in one of the passages, he let us know that it was for our benefit.

> [10]*"... The words that I say to you I do not speak on my own initiative, but the Father abiding in Me does His works. ...* [12]*Truly, truly, I say to you, he who believes in Me, the works that I do, he will do also; and greater works than these he will do; ..."*
>
> John 14:10b, 12a

Are you kidding me? We can do greater things than Jesus Christ, the Son of God? How in the world is that possible?

By faith!

We can respond to the Father the way Jesus responded—with belief and obedience to everything God initiates.

Not only does the Holy Spirit develop our character, but in these words of Jesus we see that he also reveals God's calling in our lives, from "faith to faith."

So, if God says to you, "Apologize to Jennifer," could he possibly accomplish something bigger than employee relations?

What if he says, "Keep going"? Could it be for more than just to reiterate our Bible knowledge?

And what if he says, "Tell Cathy she'll smile again"?

You know, I've gotten myself in trouble by focusing so much attention on quotes like these, as if the Holy Spirit *always* speaks in words.

I had the privilege of leading a young woman named Becky to faith in Christ. In sharing the gospel message, I had talked a lot about 'hearing from God.' She became so focused on hearing the Holy Spirit speak words to her that she called me every other day for two weeks telling me, "I haven't heard anything yet, but I can't wait until I do." I was starting to sweat bullets by the time she called and shared with me how God had told her to throw away her cigarettes, breaking her addiction to nicotine.

Whew! That was close.

But still, we need to understand that communication from God is more than just words. And because of God's purposes behind the things his Holy Spirit speaks into our lives, it's incredibly important that we learn to live by faith. *Incredibly* important?

> ⁶*And without faith it is impossible to please Him, for he who comes to God must believe that He is and that He is a rewarder of those who seek Him.*   Hebrews 11:6

> ²³*... and whatever is not from faith is sin.*   Romans 14:23b

If we're not living by faith, we're not really enjoying a friendship with God the way he intends. We're not living a life that pleases him. And we're not really experiencing the blessings he wants to give us. Quite bluntly, if we're living a life that can't be described as "a believing and obedient response to God's initiative," we're living out of bounds. We're living in sin.

The Extra Effort (Search & Rescue)

☞ <u>your name</u> *Lives by Faith*—Why does it matter? Taken at face value, what implications does this headline have for the entire human race?

....

....

....

❧ _your name_ _Lives by Faith_—What difference does it make for you? Think about these statements and summarize your response below.

- I hear, believe, and obey the Holy Spirit.
- I create _faith opportunities_ by reading the Bible, praying, and going to church.
- The Holy Spirit is addressing my character.
- He is revealing my calling.

....

....

....

*   *   *

- Where will you read in the Old Testament? The Gospels and Acts? The New Testament Letters?
- Read carefully, pray intentionally, think, question, and listen.

Time with God #1 – Old Testament   Date _____/_____/_____

What scriptures did you choose to read?
....

What did you talk to God about?
....

....

What did God say to you?
....

....

....

In what ways(s) will you respond?
....

....

Time with God #2 – The Gospels and Acts   Date _____/_____/_____

What scriptures did you choose to read?

What did you talk to God about?

What did God say to you?

In what ways(s) will you respond?

Time with God #3 – New Testament Letters   Date _____/_____/_____

What scriptures did you choose to read?

What did you talk to God about?

What did God say to you?

In what ways(s) will you respond?

* * *

☙ If you can, note a recent news story, as well as a personal story, that relates to topics in this chapter.

News:
_____

Personal:
_____

☙ List two things that impacted you as you read the chapter or participated in a group discussion.

_____

_____

_____

Scoring for *Search & Rescue* discussion groups:

*Read-4 * Notes-8 * News-1 * Personal-2 * Impact-16 * Total-_____*

[1] 1 Corinthians 11:1

[2] Proverbs 6:34-35

[3] Proverbs 6:27-29

[4] Hebrews 12:2

[5] Romans 10:17

[6] Philippians 4:7

[7] Mark 9:23

[8] Hebrews 13:8

[9] Romans 1:17

[10] 2 Corinthians 5:21

[11] 1 John 3:2

[12] Seven passages from the Gospel of John in which Jesus said that his Father in heaven initiated everything he said and did:

    1) John 5:19 & 30

    2) John 6:38

    3) John 7:16-17

    4) John 8:26, 28-29, 38, 42 & 46-47

    5) John 12:49-50

    6) John 14:11

    7) John 17:7-8

GOD AND PEOPLE, TOGETHER FOREVER

*** *Multitudes once missing reappear* *** *Where were they?* *** *Is this the end or the beginning?* ***

Mt. Olivet– Science-fiction writers could not have crafted a more incredible story than what the world has been witnessing over these last several years. Seemingly every individual who disappeared without a trace a few years ago returned to Earth today riding white horses with Jesus Christ, the King of kings and Lord

of lords. Jesus returned to earth about 2000 years after His followers claim He ascended into heaven after rising from the dead. Doubters were silenced once and for all at his appearance. Christ returned as hostile military maneuvers were taking place in the Valley of Megiddo. The nation of Israel was on high alert

at the time. leaders having called for a National Day of Prayer for Deliverance. Jesus Christ came to their rescue like he was the answer to their prayers. One can only wonder what the future holds now.
Full Story
—*Revelation 20 and 21*

Letter Postmarked 1948 Finally Delivered

By the Way, She's Singing!

14 ❧ God and People, Together Forever

A Bible Study for the Pop Charts

¹¹... He has also set eternity in their heart, ...   *Ecclesiastes 3:11b*

One morning, I woke up with a song in my head that I had been singing in a dream.

> *And the meek shall inherit the earth*
> *And the lion shall lie down with a lamb*
> *Welcome to the kingdom of God*
>
> *And he will dry their tears from their eyes*
> *And the nations shall worship the Lord*
> *And the street is paved with transparent gold*
> *Welcome to the kingdom of God*

I spent the next ten hours intently searching through the Bible for snapshots of *The Kingdom of God*. That's what I called the song when it was finished.

We will see a new heaven and earth
For the first will both pass away
We will see New Jerusalem descending
For God will be with his people on earth   *(Revelation 21:1-3)*

He will swallow up death forever
He will wipe all tears from our eyes
The rebuke of his people he will take away
For the Lord God has spoken this   *(Isaiah 25:8)*

Overcomers will inherit all things   *(Revelation 21:7)*
The King will say, "Come, blessed of My Father.   *(Matthew 25:34)*
"In My Father's house are many mansions.
"I have prepared a place just for you.   *(John 14:2)*

"The poor in spirit and the persecuted
"Will inherit the kingdom of God.   *(Matthew 5:3, 10)*
"Those who mourn will be blessed by his comfort.   *(Matthew 5:4)*
"And the meek will inherit the earth.   *(Matthew 5:5)*

"Those who hunger for right will be filled.   *(Matthew 5:6)*
"And the merciful will reap what they have sown.   *(Matthew 5:7)*
"The pure in heart will set their eyes on the Lord.   *(Matthew 5:8)*
"And those who make peace will be called his sons."   *(Matthew 5:9)*

But the wicked will know the second death
In the lake that burns with fire and brimstone   *(Revelation 21:8)*
Where the Beast, the Devil, and the False Prophet
Are tormented both day and night   *(Revelation 20:10)*

New Jerusalem will shine like precious stones
Descending out of heaven from the Lord
She has a great and high wall surrounding her
And there are twelve angels guarding her gates   *(Revelation 21:10-12)*

The city's wall sets on twelve foundations   *(Revelation 21:14)*
And each foundation is a different precious stone
Every gate is made of only one single pearl
And the city street is transparent gold   *(Revelation 21:19-21)*

The sun will no longer be the light of day
And the moon will be no longer needed there
For the Lord will be the Light everlasting
Thus, the days of our mourning will end   *(Isaiah 60:19-20)*

We will say, "Let us go to the Lord.
"He will teach us, we will walk in his way."
All the swords will be changed into plowshares
And the spears into pruning hooks   *(Isaiah 2:3-4a & Micah 4:2-3a)*

Nations will not rise against nations
And nations will not study war anymore   *(Isaiah 2:4b & Micah 4:3b)*
But everyone will sit and rest under his own tree
We will walk in the name of the Lord   *(Micah4:4-5)*

Then the eyes of the blind will see
And the ears of the deaf be unstopped
Then the lame man will leap and the mute tongue, sing
In the wilderness the waters will run   *(Isaiah 35:5-6)*

Then the virgin will rejoice in her dance
See together, the young men and old
For God will turn our mourning into glorious joy
And satisfy his people with good things   *(Jeremiah 31:13-14)*

And the wolf will live with the lamb
And the leopard will lie down with the kid
See together, the calf and the lion
And a little child will lead them   *(Isaiah 11:6)*
And a little child will lead them
And a little child will lead them

A Message of Hope and Comfort

[2]"In My Father's house are many dwelling places; if it were not so, I would have told you; for I go to prepare a place for you. [3]If I go and prepare a place for you, I will come again and receive you to Myself, that where I am, there you may be also."

John 14:2-3

Jesus Christ is coming again!

Books have been written, movies have been produced, and churches have presented dramas which suppose the harsh reality and negative emotions of "the last days." For some people, 'the end of the world' is a scary thing, but for Christians, it shouldn't be. We have nothing to fear.

We've just seen snapshots of the kingdom of God. Although there will be an end to this world as we know it, there will be no end to the world that people were created for. So, if we're involved in a friendship with God, there's absolutely no reason for us to be afraid. And it actually goes deeper than this. If our spirit has been born again and our soul is being changed to become more like Jesus, then we should be looking forward to the day that our physical bodies will also experience salvation.

> ²Beloved, now we are children of God, and it has not appeared as yet what we will be. We know that when He appears, we will be like Him, because we will see Him just as He is. ³And everyone who has this hope fixed on Him purifies himself, just as He is pure.
>
> 1 John 3:2-3

> ⁵¹Behold, I tell you a mystery; we will not all sleep, but we will all be changed, ⁵²in a moment, in the twinkling of an eye, at the last trumpet; for the trumpet will sound, and the dead will be raised imperishable, and we will be changed. ⁵³For this perishable must put on the imperishable, and this mortal must put on immortality.
>
> 1 Corinthians 15:51-53

> ¹⁵For this we say to you by the word of the Lord, that we who are alive and remain until the coming of the Lord, will not precede those who have fallen asleep. ¹⁶For the Lord Himself will descend from heaven with a shout, with the voice of the archangel and with the trumpet of God, and the dead in Christ will rise first. ¹⁷Then we who are alive and remain will be caught up together with them in the clouds to meet the Lord in the air, and so we shall always be with the Lord. ¹⁸Therefore comfort one another with these words.
>
> 1 Thessalonians 4:15-18

Bible scholars disagree on the details of Christ's return as described by the passages we've just read, but whatever the facts may be regarding this topic, we must make an important distinction very clear. John refers to Christ's return as "this hope." And Paul says that we're to bring people comfort with this message.

My dad was a student of the end times for more than 20 years. After all that time and effort, he realized that he still had more questions than he did answers. So he prayed that God would show him how all the puzzle pieces of Bible prophecy fit together. Now I have to be careful here, because it's not my intention to present one man's Bible interpretation. God answered his prayer with something special, and maybe one rainy day I'll share it with you. But here's the thing. The way that God had answered my dad's prayer was amazing to me, so amazing, in fact, that I decided to pray a similar prayer. *God, do for me what you did for my dad. Show me what the Book of Revelation is all about.*

Grinning from ear to ear, I opened my Bible to the final book and began reading. I read chapter after chapter and … nothing. There was still an excitement in my heart as I finished Chapter 18, but began thinking, "God, you've only got three chapters left."

Then I began reading Chapter 19.

¹… "Hallelujah! Salvation and glory and power belong to our God;"

Revelation 19:1b

³And a second time they said, "Hallelujah! …" ⁴And the twenty-four elders and the four living creatures fell down and worshiped God who sits on the throne saying, "Amen. Hallelujah!" ⁵And a voice came from the throne, saying,

"Give praise to our God, all you His bond-servants, you who fear Him, the small and the great." ⁶Then I heard something like the voice of a great multitude and like the sound of many waters and like the sound of mighty peals of thunder, saying, "Hallelujah! For the Lord our God, the Almighty, reigns. ⁷Let us rejoice and be glad and give the glory to Him, …"

Revelation 19:3a, 4-7a

¹⁰"… worship God. For the testimony of Jesus is the spirit of prophecy."

¹¹And I saw heaven opened, and behold, a white horse, and He who sat on it is called Faithful and True, and in righteousness He judges and wages war. ¹²His eyes are a flame of fire, and on His head are many diadems; and He has a name written on Him which no one knows except Himself. ¹³He is clothed with a robe dipped in blood, and His name is called The Word of God. ¹⁴And the armies which are in heaven, clothed in fine linen, white and clean, were following Him on white horses.

Revelation 19:10b-14

¹⁶And on His robe and on His thigh He has a name written, "KING OF KINGS, AND LORD OF LORDS."

Revelation 19:16

At that very moment—*"King of kings, and Lord of lords"*—the Holy Spirit spoke, and this entire analogy came to me.

The President of the United States is going to make an important speech in my home city. For this visit and any other like it, there's a protocol that everyone follows.

- Air Force One will land on a certain runway at the airport at a certain time.
- The President and his security detail will disembark from the plane in a specific order.
- The President will be received by a specific contingency of dignitaries.
- Certain members of the press will be allowed to document the moment.
- The Presidential motorcade will leave the airport at a precise time.
- Certain stretches of highway and inner city intersections will be barricaded and guarded by state and local law enforcement.
- The Presidential party will come into the convention center at a precise time via a secured entrance.
- The President will be introduced by a notable personality and will step onto the stage at a precise time.

I understood from what the Holy Spirit was showing me that the President's *itinerary* is important, but not as important as the President's *appearance*. The Book of Revelation is a description of events, an itinerary if you will, preceding the return of Jesus Christ. The details of the itinerary are not as important as the fact that one day Jesus will appear and be *revealed* to all of humanity as the King of kings and Lord of lords—period. (This is why the book is called Revelation, rather than Revelation*s*.)

And here's the crazy thing. My dad and I received completely different types of answers from God, but the answers we received satisfied each of us. I don't know that either one of us was so wrapped up in figuring out the future after that. I know that the symbolism of Bible prophecy is strange, and I'm well aware that there are some tough days that lie ahead for people. (That's an understatement.) But, for me, the need to know who the Antichrist will be disappeared when the message became hopeful and comforting.

The Future Pulls on Today

[11]*For the grace of God has appeared, bringing salvation to all men,* [12]*instructing us to deny ungodliness and worldly desires and to live sensibly, righteously and godly in the present age,* [13]*looking for the blessed hope and the appearing of the glory of our great God and Savior, Christ Jesus, ..."*   Titus 2:11-13

There's a connection between the future that we Christians look forward to and our lives here and now. We are to live appropriately in the present age, as we look forward. Wise King Solomon wrote:

> *13The conclusion, when all has been heard, is: fear God and keep His commandments, because this applies to every person. 14For God will bring every act to judgment, everything which is hidden, whether it is good or evil.*
>
> *Ecclesiastes 12:13-14*

Of course, what I'm talking about is commonly known as Judgment Day.

Although Bible scholars discuss as many as three judgments for humanity and as few as only one, most agree that there are at least two different 'Judgment Days' described in the Bible.

There's one for non-Christians before God's great white throne that is based on a single question: Is your name written in the book of life? We'll talk more about this later. And there's a different judgment for Christians, before the judgment seat of Christ.

Whenever I mention a Judgment Day for Christians, the question is almost always asked, "How can Christians be judged if Jesus already paid the penalty for our sins?"

That's a great question. And the answer is simple; it isn't a judgment to determine punishment for sin; rather, it determines rewards for our faithfulness.

> *10For we must all appear before the judgment seat of Christ, so that each one may be <u>recompensed</u> for his deeds in the body, according to what he has done, whether good or bad.*
>
> *2 Corinthians 5:10*

The question asked of Christians before the judgment seat of Christ will be: *Since* your name is in the book of life, what did you do with the life Jesus gave you? What did you build on the foundation of Christ in your life?

> *12Now if any man builds on the foundation with gold, silver, precious stones, wood, hay, straw, 13each man's work will become evident; for the day will show it because it is to be revealed with fire, and the fire itself will test the quality of each man's work. 14If any man's work which he has built on it remains, he will receive a reward. 15If any man's work is burned up, he will **suffer loss**; but he himself will be saved, yet so as through fire.*
>
> *1 Corinthians 3:12-15* [emphasis added]

I've known some Christian people who lived as though Jesus died to make sin okay, rather than to make sinners righteous.

> [28]*Now, little children, abide in Him, so that when He appears, we may have confidence and not* **shrink away** *from Him* **in shame** *at His coming.*
>
> *1 John 2:28* [emphasis added]

Suffer loss? Shrink away in shame? In the kingdom of God?

Sometimes, I catch myself doing something I know I shouldn't do. Whenever I see a Christian behaving poorly—

I mean, it happens, right? The most common accusation against Christians is that we're hypocrites. We say one thing and do another.

Whenever I see a Christian really blow it, I can't help but think, *Doesn't that person know that he'll stand before God and be held accountable?* That sounds judgmental, doesn't it? It might help to know that the Christian I'm referring to is me.

At this point, I'm thinking of my own life and imagining a chunk of Swiss cheese; gaping holes where my time, my thoughts, and my actions were wasted on things I hoped I wouldn't get caught doing. But according to the Bible, I'm already caught.

You see, I'm convinced, beyond any shadow of a doubt, that I'll stand before Jesus one day. And I know that, among all of the other moments that we'll talk about, he'll ask, "Eric, what did you do when, on a snowy Saturday night in October of 1989, I told you to stand up and stop a false prophet?"

What if he has me cup my hands together and hold this moment? I'm standing there staring at a moment that God had great plans for, while he sits there silently, waiting for my answer.

There's the false prophet. There's my nervous leg. There's my head shaking no. And Jesus simply waits.

After an embarrassingly painful silence, I have no choice but to respond, "I'm sorry, Lord, I disobeyed you." In a sudden puff of smoke, ashes fall through my fingers.

I don't believe that I'll take 39 lashes across my back, or that I'll be crucified for losing this moment. The penalty for my sin really has been paid.

I believe that I've come to terms with this moment and that I've shared it with others in a way that honors God ... many times.

But whatever God intended this moment to be—all those years ago—has been lost.

"Eric."

I bow my head before Jesus.

"What did you do when, on a misty Saturday morning in October of 2002, I told you to tell Cathy she'll smile again?"

I smile and look into my hands to see this special moment, but instead I find a piece of gold, a chunk of silver, or a precious stone.

"Well done, good and faithful servant."

I don't share this little scene as though I've seen heaven and I know what things will be like. I really have no clue. I share it with you because it lives inside my heart and mind. It pulls on me.

And these words, *well done, good and faithful servant*—I want to hear God speak these words concerning my life. And I know that all I have to do is live the life that Jesus Christ gave me when I was only 5½ years old. All I have to do is do well in letting God develop his goodness in me, do well in making my life a faithful response to his Holy Spirit, and do well in serving God and others. That's all I have to do.

It's not only the future that pulls on me to do this. There's something from the past that pushes me forward me as well.

> "Well done, good and faithful servant. You were faithful with a few things, I will put you in charge of many things; enter into the joy of your master."
>
> —*Jesus Christ*

> *⁴¹... [Jesus] knelt down and began to pray, ⁴²saying, "Father, if you are willing, remove this cup from Me; yet not My will, but Yours be done." ⁴³Now an angel from heaven appeared to Him, strengthening Him. ⁴⁴And being in agony He was praying very fervently; and His sweat became like drops of blood, falling down upon the ground.*
>
> Luke 22:41b-44

I imagine Jesus praying this prayer, pushed to the brink. I see him helped to his feet afterwards, having 100% commitment in his eyes. He's determined to carry out my rescue, to save me, to give me a life with God that should have been lost forever. And suddenly, I remember that my reward of gold, silver, and precious stones will equal my gratitude for his willingness not to lose me.

In Revelation 4:10 we see a picture of people falling down before God and worshipping him. We see them surrendering their crowns at his feet. I want to do that. I want to place my reward—whatever it may be—at his feet and worship him for loving me.

> *¹¹Worthy are You, our Lord and our God, to receive glory and honor and power; for You created all things, and because of Your will they existed, and were created."*
>
> Revelation 4:11

More than anything, I don't want my life to be an insult to God's grace.

Starting Over and Finishing Strong

You know, I've tried to over-fill this book with stories from my life with God to show others that they, too, can experience the kind of friendship with God that over-fills books. Quite honestly, I want everyone's life to be a testament to God's grace rather than an insult. After all, Jesus didn't die for just a select few. He died for all of us.

> *9... "Worthy are You ...; for You were slain, and purchased for God with Your blood men from every tribe and tongue and people and nation.*
> *10You have made them to be a kingdom and priests to our God; and they will reign upon the earth."*
>
> Revelation 5:9-10

God's intention from the beginning, his foreseen history with people, was to rescue us and give us himself forever. This is why I know with complete certainty that I (and you, if you so choose) will be one of the:

> *11... myriads of myriads, and thousands of thousands, saying with a loud voice,*
>
> *"Worthy is the Lamb that was slain to receive power and riches and wisdom and might and honor and glory and blessing."*
>
> *And every created thing which is in heaven and on the earth and under the earth and on the sea, and all things in them, I heard saying,*
>
> *"To Him who sits on the throne, and to the Lamb, be blessing and honor and glory and dominion forever and ever."*
>
> Revelation 5:11b-13

Will I be ready for this magnificent moment? Will you?

The Extra Effort (Search & Rescue)

❧ *God and People, Together Forever*—Why does it matter? Taken at face value, what implications does this headline have for the entire human race?

❧ *God and People, Together Forever*—What difference does it make for you? Think about these statements and summarize your response below.
- I look forward to Christ's return.
- I know that I will be judged and rewarded for doing well in goodness, faithfulness, and my service to God.
- I feel the pull of the kingdom of God in my life.

* * *

❧ If you can, note a recent news story, as well as a personal story, that relates to topics in this chapter.

News:

Personal:

❧ List two things that impacted you as you read the chapter or participated in a group discussion.

_____

_____

_____

Scoring for *Search & Rescue* discussion groups:

Read-4 ∗ Notes-8 ∗ News-1 ∗ Personal-2 ∗ Impact-16 ∗ Total-_____

SOME PEOPLE REJECT GOD

It was never meant to be this way. ✱✱✱ *Apparently, everyone had a choice.* ✱✱✱

Some people reject God ...

GOD CREATES PEOPLE

*... despite the fact that he created us
to experience friendship with him.*

PEOPLE SIN AGAINST GOD

... continuing to purposefully sin against him.

GOD'S LAW IS GIVEN

... lobbying to keep his laws separate from ours.

JESUS CHRIST DIES

*... though he demonstrated his love for us
by dying in our place.*

JESUS, ALIVE AGAIN:

... working too hard to explain an empty tomb.

ACCEPTS SALVATION

*... mocking gospel ministers
who reach out to them in love.*

LIVES BY FAITH

... denying millions of changed lives.

GOD AND PEOPLE, TOGETHER FOREVER

*... despite the fact
that he will accept their choice to reject him.*

❧ Some People Reject God

This is not a great wonder. It's the flipside of eternity. It has absolutely nothing to do with Christians ... except for the fact that people we know and love are headed in this direction.

One of the most dangerous philosophies known to mankind says that because God is love, he won't be able to force people, his most-cherished creation, into hell. The error of this thought is found in this: God isn't the one who makes the decision regarding damnation. We do. Are we dead ... or alive?

> [11]*Then I saw a great white throne and Him who sat upon it, from whose presence earth and heaven fled away, and no place was found for them.* [12]*And I saw the dead, the great and the small, standing before the throne, and books were opened; and another book was opened, which is the book of life; and the dead were judged from the things which were written in the books, according to their deeds.* [13]*And the sea gave up the dead which were in it, and death and Hades gave up the dead which were in them; and they were judged, every one of them according to their deeds.* [14]*Then death and Hades were thrown into the lake of fire. This is the second death, the lake of fire.* [15]*And if anyone's name was not found written in the book of life, he was thrown into the lake of fire.*
>
> Revelation 20:11-15

I began Chapter 12 with the story of my last visit with my granddad. He died three days after our unfinished conversation about God. Prior to that day, I had written an unfinished song about him, as well as a good friend of mine, which I want to use as a lead-in to the last story in this book.

My granddad is a good ole boy
Eighty years old with a young man's mind
In all that time, he must've been told
Better do it now 'cause there ain't much time

Would I love to see him love the Lord!
Would I love to see him love the Lord!

My friend lives in Globe, Arizona
Rents a little house on the side of a hill
Once or twice, I know I've told him
You'd better do it now, or you never will

Would I love to see him love the Lord!
Would I love to see him love the Lord!

The day I met Del, my friend mentioned in the song, we played basketball through the V of a tree in my front yard.

He bought my first two packs of Elvis Presley trading cards for me. I still owe him 30¢.

He teased me a million times for an embarrassing comment I made when I was a foolish 13-year-old.

He respected the 'closed drapes' when my family's house church was in session, and the streetlight which signaled that it was time for me to go inside for the night.

Before e-mail, he used to send me the most colorful, creative, and hilarious letters. I still have every one of them.

He was one of my groomsmen.

We shared the experience of not one, but two, Paul McCartney concerts.

His family treated mine to an Iowa Cubs baseball game.

Music was our common bond. We wrote 13 songs together, and Del once wrote a song on his own that had numerous references to our musical relationship. In part, the lyric reads:

All the boys danced—all the girls sang
Was it heart or soul, back in '84?

While rest the world beat to a drummer, I was reading
My lyric lines from All the Classic Faces
And I still don't understand the concept
I still don't understand romance
Still don't understand confusion
Don't understand the vision, the reason,
The black and white of Semloh Cire, like the grey
Of life was parted with a guiding light

I think you get the idea; there's great history between us.

In February of 2004, I attended the satellite broadcast of an interview regarding the movie *The Passion of the Christ*. Afterwards, I sensed that God was leading me to take Del to see the movie once it was released. You see, for most of his adult life, Del was sometimes agnostic, sometimes atheistic in his belief about God. This movie presented what I believed to be the opportunity of a lifetime. I just knew that God was speaking to me about the movie.

In March, we saw *The Passion of the Christ* together. Afterwards, we were joined by his wife and their two small children for dinner. We talked about family, friends, life in general, and we talked about the movie. Del shared his observations. I shared my insights; that the death of Jesus was meant for me, that his death in my place demonstrated his love for me. He told me that this was worth thinking about. I also shared stories of what God had been doing in my life. Del was polite and respectful, but I could tell that he wasn't ready.

In June, we spoke on the telephone, and I asked Del where he stood with Christ. He said that he had 'prayed the sinner's prayer' several times in his life, but when it came to actual belief in Jesus Christ, he still wasn't sure.

"Fair enough. But I want you to know something. I want to be the person you talk to when you have questions."

"If I have any questions, I'll call you."

You know, it didn't seem like it at first, but maybe the movie had done exactly what I knew God wanted it to do. We were talking about issues of faith more openly than at any other time in our friendship. I was looking forward to the possibilities of where this might be leading.

On July 12th, Del's cell phone number appeared on my caller ID, but it was a co-worker of his named Tim.

"You're a friend of Del's, aren't you?"

"Absolutely."

"Eric ... Del was killed in a car wreck this morning."

It was never about the movie.

Eric Holmes Ministries

Eric Holmes Ministries is a 501(c)(3) nonprofit corporation, a Christian ministry that teaches the dynamics of a real relationship with God to non-religious and religious people alike. This evangelistic discipleship ministry has been "leading people to a knowledge of purpose and a calling of service" since 2003, with the goal of helping all people to *hear the music of God's voice* for themselves rather than *deafly imitating the snaps and taps of Christians* around them.

"There's no greater feeling than the one that comes when someone you've shared the message with is filled with excitement because God has spoken to them directly. There's no greater satisfaction than knowing that your small part had something to do with Jesus becoming the Lord of another person's life."

—Eric Holmes

E-mail comments and questions to: **Faith@EricHolmesMinistries.org**

Printed in the United States
63093LVS00001B/119-1506